4-53

A PENNY FROM HEAVEN

A
Penny
from
Heaven

BY

Max Winkler

APPLETON-CENTURY-CROFTS, INC.
New York

A PENNY FROM HEAVEN

1.

Today is Thanksgiving Day. It's a bright, brisk morning. There are still a few leaves on the elm tree down in the garden. The sky is clear. It's quiet outside. No traffic noise, no trucks, even the train whistles are few and far between. It's a holiday.

Thanksgiving Day is one of the few holidays of the year when I not only don't go to work but don't even think about business. I have so much to be thankful for that one day in the year seems never to be enough to absorb all my thoughts of gratitude and all my memories, sad and bitter, gay and bright.

My name is Max Winkler. I am a music publisher. I have a business, a house, a family. I am an American citizen. I came to this country many years ago from the mountains of Carpathia, near the Eastern border of Austria, with nothing but my two hands and my two arms. It has been a very hard and a very happy life. Today, as I look back on it in the quiet hour of Thanksgiving morning, I know that it could have been anybody's life. Anybody's in America, that is.

Through the open door I hear the bustle downstairs in the kitchen where Clara, my wife, is preparing the dinner. Soon our children will be here. They all are married and they will come to share

1

the festive meal with us and with their own children, my grandchildren. Grandchildren! And it seems only yesterday that I stepped ashore, a boy of eighteen, fresh from the lumberyards of Rumania.

Now I hear a car. That is Martin, one of my sons. He is now a partner in my publishing business. There he steps out, I can see him through the windows— and there is his wife and little Bruce and Judy. They enter the house.

There is still a lot of time before the turkey is ready and before the other children arrive and we all sit down to give thanks. The children too, I think, the big and the small ones, will have a prayer in their hearts and a silent thought of thanksgiving. But theirs has been a friendly, a well-protected life. The house and the elm tree, the car that brought them here and the schoolhouse and the drugstore at the corner and all the freedom and happiness of their lives— they take it all for granted. It has always been theirs. But it hasn't always been mine. To me, it is still a startling gift from heaven. That's why I don't go downstairs yet. I still want to sit for a little while and think and remember. This is my own Thanksgiving hour. I have to close the door. I want to be alone for a while.

Thanksgiving Day here in Lynbrook, Long Island, U.S.A. How could it ever happen? You won't find the town where I was born on any map. I still keep my old Austrian passport somewhere in a drawer of my desk. Otherwise I couldn't even remember the name of my birthplace myself. Here it is. The Imperial

Eagle is fading on the worn-out smudgy cover. Birthplace: Riszka, Bucovina. Date of Birth: March 15,
1888.

I still remember Riszka. It was a village without
streets and squares, without a church steeple and
without a schoolhouse. It had no railroad station and
if you wanted to mail a letter or buy a pair of shoes
you had to travel four hours by carriage to the next
town. But nobody in Riszka had to mail a letter and
as for shoes, there was, at least for the younger generation, no need to make a special trip. We never
wore any in the summer, and in the winter they were
passed on, year after year, from the older to the
younger children.

The population of our town varied from seventeen
to fifty-one. There were my father and my mother,
there were Dave, my twin brother, and I, there were
brothers Jack and Herman and sister Rose, the baby.
That accounted for seven of our citizens. The remain-
der were Herr Kolmetz, the cashier, a couple of
Verwalters and *Unterverwalters* with their *Frau Verwalters* and *Frau Unterverwalters,* and Frau Wasserbart, a strong, towering matron who was the town's
doctor, barber, midwife, druggist and master of Herr
Wasserbart, her pint-sized husband who operated
the general store. Herr Wasserbart was a great and
never-tiring attraction to us children. An overpowering affinity to the potato schnapps which he used to
bring once a week in a barrel from the distant town
of Foltiszenhi—"Much too good to be sold," he used
to say to my father—had so greatly affected his throat

that he had lost his voice completely and had to go off to Vienna for medical advice. Everybody thought he would never come back but would succumb to the supplies of potato schnapps that must be inexhaustible in so famous a city. But miraculously he returned with a silver tube in his throat. If you begged him long enough he would take it out and show it to an admiring circle of fans. He was now immune to potato schnapps, and the fiery beverage disappeared forever from the articles on sale in our general store.

Of the seven or eight frame buildings that comprised the town which nestled deep in the Carpathian Mountains of Bucovina (a strip of land that was then a part of the Austro-Hungarian Empire but was annexed by Rumania after the first World War and by Russia after the second), the nicest was the one our family lived in. Even so it was a strictly one-story affair; it had no cellar and when the rains swept down in the autumn and the snow began to melt in the spring the water came rushing into our rooms, carrying moss and pebbles and countless black beetles that would remain long after the flood had receded and would crawl eerily and with rattling noise around our uneasy beds. The beds had mattresses made of burlap and filled with straw. When the straw was fresh you had the feeling of lying in a noisy stack of hay. After about two or three hundred turns, more churns than turns, the long stems of the straw slowly broke up into millions of little pieces. They gave you the feeling of sleeping on a bag of cornflakes. A few hundred turns later and the cornflakes turned into little hard grapenuts. Sleeping on grapenuts had one advantage, you had no trouble scratching your back. All you had to do was to roll over several times.

But what our town lacked in comfort and grandeur it made up by its location and surroundings. For miles and miles on end the mountains and valleys were covered with sprawling forests: pine trees, dark, tall, green, and beautiful. The ground was a thick carpet of soft needles. Bears and foxes, deer and rabbits lived nearby and we boys knew their trails and scents and drinking places. The unforgettable aroma of the pine trees, of moss and bark, of dew and sunshine filled our lungs.

My father had come here as manager of a big sawmill.

The word sawmill, if you think of our own mountains of Vermont or Oregon or Wisconsin, brings to the mind a wheezing, sparkling assembly of glittering blades, of huge trees being rushed through a streamlined co-ordination of knives, of pines transformed within a matter of seconds into neat stacks of boards.

I have none of these associations when I think of our sawmill. Our town had no electric current. No roads penetrated the valleys and the peaks. Five thousand men had to work to keep our mill going. Most of them came from surrounding villages. Others had made our town their permanent domicile. There they slept in *kolibas*, tents rigged up on poles like Indian tents, each housing some twenty or

thirty men. The work went on twenty-four hours a
day for a six-day week and in these twenty-four
hours there were only two shifts. The day shift began
at five in the morning and ended at seven at night.
There was a thirty-minute interruption for breakfast
and another thirty minutes for lunch. The night shift
lasted from seven to five. Everybody hated the day
shift—it was unbearably long; and everybody hated
the night shift because it was hard, cold and dangerous. At four in the morning a steam siren would
blow for ten terrifying minutes to make sure that
everyone was on time for the morning shift. I still
can hear it today, after almost sixty years, screaming through my dreams.

Only a few hundred of the men worked in the
mill. The others, thousands of them, were scattered
through the woods, cutting trees with saw and ax,
chopping off branches, peeling off bark and, at last,
hauling the trunks with their bare hands to crevasses
where they would be stored till snow and ice made
a natural slide on which they came crashing down
by their own power. The last stretch to the mill was
negotiated by our own railroad that wound its asthmatic course up some six miles into the mountains.
A little steam engine pulled the empty cars uphill.
There they were loaded and then released for the
downward trip under their own power, five men on
each car frantically trying to operate the brakes. Far
behind that mad chase of swaying cars, tumbling
logs, screaming brakes and shouting men came the
lonesome engine, puffing lustily and relieved down-

hill. I have often made that horrifying trip. When I later met Coney Island's wildest roller coasters I boarded them with a contemptuous smile.

These were the surroundings of my early days: the woods, the mill, a town without a schoolhouse, the men working their fourteen-hour shift, the little railroad and, on Sunday, the men, those who hadn't gone home to their own villages, drinking, dancing, and fighting. A fiddle made its appearance at the little green in front of the general store, joined sometimes by a cymbalo or a clarinet. The men sang and danced the *Hora* and the *Sirba*, forming a wide circle, stamping the ground as they held on to each other's arms till at last the schnapps became mightier than the music, the first fights broke out, the musicians began to run, trying to save their instruments, and my mother came rushing out of the house to take us home.

Here in our own village, and for miles and miles throughout the mountains, my father was king, ruling with an iron hand over his five thousand workers, over his wife and over five children that had learned very early in life—and had learned it the hard, the old-fashioned way—who was the boss in the house. My mother was a fine and gentle person, the kind of mother who would hide unknown to us behind a window curtain to watch us boys at play, looking after us until we disappeared from her sight. She was devoted to my father to a degree which I have never encountered again. He was her lord. She never offered any defense. She just listened and smiled. She never tried to make any decision: she would even send one of us children into the woods to ask father whether she was to cook peas or beans for dinner.

Once in a while, however, even Father had to strip off the king's mantle, had to take off his hat, and bow. These were the days when the owner of the mill arrived for one of his visits to the great outdoors. Unannounced—there wouldn't have been any means of announcing his visit anyway—he would arrive in a magnificent four-horse carriage, with coachman and footmen, with his wife and children (five sons and two daughters), and move at once into our little house. We children would spend the ensuing days that many times stretched into weeks, in barns or in one of the big tents where the men slept heavily after their hard day's work and where the big log fires roasted our feet while our heads froze in the biting chill of the mountains. We had, however, one consolation. The thought that the five noble sons and two refined daughters were turning uneasily on our beds of grapenuts made our dreams pleasant, smooth and content.

The visitors ate heartily at 7 A.M. and not less heartily at 1 and at 8 P.M.—no one in these golden days had heard of a diet and the mountain air still increased their enormous appetites. There had to be a second breakfast at ten (although they certainly had no fast to break) and a snack with coffee and cream and a half a dozen *butterbrote* per head at four in the afternoon. They never paid a penny.

As suddenly as they had arrived they packed up

again and left. Father watched the carriage totter
down the dusty road. Then he turned and cracked
his stick at some of the loafers who in the excitement
had missed a few minutes of their shift. The king
was back on his throne.

It was a rough but a happy life, a good life—and
as do all good things it had to come to an end. The
end came on a beautiful crisp day in December, 1897.
Brother Dave and I—with Jack, Herman, and the
baby as an admiring audience—were just passing a
busy afternoon at our favorite sport: throwing stones
so high in the air that they would fall into the sawmill chimney. It was a wonderful sport. About one
out of every three hundred stones made it. The other
299 came crashing down over a wide area, threatening the lives of man and beast. The beasts—geese,
dogs, cats and goats—fled in screaming terror and
man took in silent fury what was coming to him from
the sons of the mighty *Herr Verwalter.* As far as we
were concerned all we knew was that we got hungry
about every three hundred stones.

But on that fateful December day (we had
celebrated shortly before our ninth birthday) our
mighty pitching contest came to an abrupt end.
Father's voice was heard from the house. As we arrived with the breathless speed that every one of
my father's commands would invariably produce he
told us that tomorrow morning at four he was to
take us to Radautz, a country town some hundred
miles away. We were to live there with my mother's
parents and were to attend school. Father's decisions

were never subject to questioning or discussion. We looked at Mother in a futile search for help but she sadly smiled her sweet timid smile and went silently back to her kitchen. The next morning at 3:55 precisely two tired, shivering, and very frightened little boys bid a tearful good-by to a tearful mother. Father was already calling impatiently from the sleigh. The coachman cracked his whip. The horses, steaming in the early frost, broke into a sharp trot. The house, the mill, the mountains of my childhood disappeared forever in the misty night.

Radautz, a county center of some twenty thousand inhabitants, with a courthouse, a big white church and a detachment of His Imperial Majesty's Yellow Dragons, made a tremendous impression on us. For the first time we saw a two-story house, a policeman, a drugstore. For hours we would linger in front of a delicatessen, taking in the confusing smells of unknown spices, looking at food in the windows—food which we had never tasted and which we couldn't even name. The streets were wide and filled with people, horses and carts. Thursday was market day and the town seemed to burst its seams. Early in the morning the peasants from faraway villages began to arrive. Their ox and horse carts crowded the market square and spilled over into every street of the town. They were loaded with children, wives, vegetables, wood, fowl, flowers, flour and eggs. Everybody heckled, hollered, traded, exchanged goods, words, jokes, and insults. Some even bought and paid for things.

About an hour before sunset the colorful caravan started on its homeward trek. By now the peasants were tired and thirsty. They had money under their belts and ever so often on their way home they would stop for refreshments and for a last noisy contact with the high life of the city. Grandpa and Grandma operated a *Wirtshaus und Trafik* in their house, a combination of store, drugstore and bar where Grandma sold schnapps, pretzels and tobacco. On Thursday she sold very few pretzels and an awful lot of schnapps. The place was then filled with Hungarians, Rumanians, Lithuanians, and German-speaking Austrians. By the time the sun disappeared in the west the Hungarians didn't like the Rumanians, the Austrians were mad at the Poles, the Lithuanians, using knives and chairs as their means of persuasion, tried to make peace. In the midst of pandemonium Grandma appeared. Within five minutes peace was restored. Within ten minutes the place was empty.

Yes, Grandma was a great fighter—in her *Wirtshaus* as well as in her home. To us who had grown up in the awe-inspiring presence of a dominating, stick-wielding man the presence of a dominating, stick-wielding woman was a shocking novelty. It was a complete reversal of what we had accepted as one of the basic laws of human relations. Something was wrong with Grandma's feet: she always limped, always used a walking stick, and always was mad and cranky. A limping cranky woman with a stick is the worst combination in the world, particularly for two young boys who through all their rough mountain lives had still retained a certain sensitiveness in the lower parts of their backs.

Dave and I made friends and enemies very fast. We were two wild strong kids, full of fight and mischief. Nine years of inhaling the balsam of the pines, of outdoor life, of the coasting rides on our railroad, had given us the strength, stamina and courage that soon put respect into the heads of our new schoolmates. We were identical twins and it didn't take us long to figure out that "two heads are better than one," particularly if both heads look absolutely alike. Soon we were able to turn this old maxim into enjoyable profits.

Students as well as teachers were able to identify us only by our locations in the classroom. Everybody knew that the big fellow in the fifth row was Max and the fellow in the ninth (just as big, just as wild, just as unkempt) was Dave. I was very good in mathematics and in German. Dave was a fine though not a great scholar of Latin and geography. The system in our school made it possible for every student to know well in advance on which day and in what subject he would be called for oral examination. When we filed into our classrooms on one of these dreaded days, who could notice that Dave smilingly took my seat in row five while I was innocently drifting towards row nine? Nobody could and nobody ever did. The result was a brilliant record for Dave in mathematics and German, subjects in which he knew absolutely nothing, while I worked up a splendid scale of marks in geography and in Latin, a language which to this day has remained a deep enigma to me.

There were grave reasons for these strenuous efforts to achieve the best possible results in school. Twice a year my parents came regularly to Radautz to visit us. While Mother retired to Grandma's kitchen to prepare some special delicacies for us, some of the things that only a mother can cook to the taste of a boy, Father paid his visit to the school. When he came home he was satisfied but not surprised. The two boys of Herr Verwalter Winkler, in his opinion, could only do excellently. We never told him how we had arrived at all this undeserved glory and even today I would not dare to write it down on paper if he were still with us.

After his successful visit to the school Father took all of us, Mother, Dave and myself, for an outing. There was usually a sideshow somewhere in the outskirts of town, or a circus, and we proudly climbed in his carriage and drove through the town, scornfully shouting at our playmates and trying to impress them with the magnificence of our entourage. First we would stop somewhere for a *Jause,* an afternoon *Kaffeklatsch* with cakes and pies and whipped cream, and then proceed to the circus. Herr Bernhard Winkler was in town—and nothing was too good or too expensive.

I have often, much later when I began to earn my own pennies and dimes on the cruel sidewalks of New York, marveled at the grandiose system by which my father handled his financial affairs. He never had a bank account and my mother never saw or even touched any money. As for us boys, the only way to get even the most pitiful token of pocket money was to blackmail Grandpa by crowding around him when he was talking to his cronies in the midst of the busy market place and asking him for a kreutzer, an amount in Austrian currency too infinitesimal to be translated into American money. Grandpa would throw a tormented look at the two innocent-looking beggars, search his huge pockets for the two kreutzers and hand them over, murder in his eyes. When we came home, later, the holdup had already been reported to Grandma and prompt corporal punishment followed the crime. Not even Grandma's stick however could take the candy out of our stomachs and the satisfying feeling of a good day's work from our minds. Crime, I am grieved to say, had paid.

But to come back to Father's financial organization. Once a month his salary arrived by messenger. He would empty the bag of coins on a big table and then the door of our living room—it was called the Salon—would be opened. In came a procession of mountain merchants—butcher, grocer, Herr Wasserbart from the general store or his mighty spouse—presenting little slips of paper signed by my mother and indicating in scarcely decipherable hieroglyphs

what she had purchased during the previous month.
Father began paying and continued till the little hill
of coins was gone. All the time he kept on commenting on the extravagance of his wife, and my mother
listened patiently, never even trying to explain
where all this meat, fowl, wurst and bread had gone.
The merchants always seemed quite happy. They
had known the routine for years and knew that eventually everybody's turn would come. I would have
occasion, many years later and under very different
surroundings, to remember not without some misgivings my father's approach towards the problems
of finance.

For the biannual visits to Radautz, however,
enough money was always set aside to make these
trips memorable and impressive events. It was at
one of these visits that—as it happened so many times
in my life later on—fate seemed to take a kindly interest in my unimportant affairs. We had gone to the
circus again. A group of Ashantis, very dark, very
tall savages from Central Africa, was then the big
attraction. Nobody in Radautz had ever seen a Negro
before and these men, women and children, scantily
and fancifully dressed, were a great experience. Just
when we left, a gypsy approached my father.

"You have two fine boys here, *Herr Baron,*" he said.
He must have been a fine student of psychology, that
gypsy. Father at once assumed the majestic attitude
of the successful king of the mountains. "They are
fine boys," the gypsy continued, "and they'll go far

in the world. They'll have money and success. But they need something to make them really happy. Here is a fiddle. Buy it for one of your boys. You'll buy happiness."

I don't know what made me do it—I had never known any music but the scream of the four o'clock steam whistle and the songs of the birds in our woods. But before Father or Dave could speak up I said, "Father, please buy me the fiddle."

Herr Verwalter Bernhard Winkler would not be shamed by a gypsy and a boy. He took out his purse, a huge black leather bag, and without asking for the price or bothering to bargain, handed the gypsy a shiny five-gulden piece.

This fiddle has been my cherished possession for fifty years. The gypsy had been right. I practiced my fiddle as a little boy and what it taught me has helped me immeasurably in my life. I don't play it any more these days. But I still keep it in the house, up in the attic, a token of luck, beauty and happiness.

Music was not the only digression from the straight path that had been mapped out for me. Love, too, had entered my life. Her name was Hulda. She was a redhead and I had fallen in love with her the first day I had seen her, when Dave and I entered school. What then had been a childish affection soon grew into a young boy's ardent love. I never looked at any other girl. Hulda was all I cared for and soon I began telling her about the day when we would both be old enough to get married. Whenever Dave or I got up at the examination in school to answer every question in a blaze of glory, Hulda looked happy and proud: not even she was able to notice the substitution and so I cashed in handsomely on an incredible accumulation of wisdom and knowledge that must have made a deep impression on a girl of twelve. Then, one day, Hulda came to school, flushed and excited. Her parents had decided to leave Radautz. The family was going, of all places, to America. I was crushed beyond description. Even Dave with his imposing knowledge of geography could only say that America was very far away.

"Even farther than Vienna?" I asked. I remembered that people had talked for months about Herr Wasserbart's trip to Vienna. It seemed at the end of the world.

"Much, much farther," Dave said.

"How far?"

He couldn't say. He made a gesture that seemed to comprise the universe.

Soon the day of departure arrived. A large crowd of friends and relatives had assembled at the railroad station. As I saw Hulda disappear in the car, waiting in vain for her to turn back once more and wave at me, I turned around. A boy of fourteen doesn't cry in public, damn it. But as I walked back towards the town that had suddenly become empty and small and meaningless I was revived by an electrifying thought.

If Hulda could go to America, so could I. I didn't have a kreutzer to myself. I didn't even know exactly where America was. But I was suddenly filled with a boundless confidence in my luck and an invigorating determination to make my life a success. I went home to my tiny room in Grandma's house and took out the gypsy's fiddle. The tune I played didn't sound sad any more. It sounded clear, sweet and strong.

2.

Two years after Hulda's departure our school days in Radautz came to an end. We were sixteen years of age now. During the final examinations a strict routine of controls completely frustrated our time-honored system of substituting for each other and thus our achievements in most of the subjects where we had excelled so brilliantly in the past became suddenly a deeply confusing disappointment to our teachers. We squeezed through, however, bade a grateful good-by to Grandpa and Grandma and boarded a train back home, seven years older and two feet taller than when we had traveled the same stretch in the opposite direction. At the station in Foltizenhi Father was waiting for us. He told us without losing time for sentimentalities that the next morning we were to begin work in the woods.

I had been assigned a job as foreman of a section gang made up of some three hundred of the strongest and meanest Rumanian lumberjacks ever to fell a tree. They hadn't seen a barber, taken a bath, or changed their clothes in many, many a month. Each man wore a leather belt some eighteen inches wide where he stored tobacco, money and at least two knives of bayonet size. Winter was approaching and the men had to be driven into unceasing efforts to

19

finish their tasks before snow made further progress impossible. I had to do the driving and they hated me with all the savage, primitive hate of primitive savages, a hatred increased by the feeling that I was a slicker who had just returned from the city and, to top it all, the son of a boss whose stern methods had failed to erect an altar of brotherly love in the hearts of his men. That I wasn't killed by one of the trees that "accidentally" fell my way or thrown off one of the coasting railroad cars seems a miracle to this day. However, after I had gotten into a real fight with one of the strongest and meanest of the gang, had made him drop his bayonet and, in a final superhuman effort of fury and defiance, had thrown him seven yards into an icy mountain pool, my position and the measure of my safety improved remarkably. Later on, when I had to wrestle much more civilized but even stronger and meaner forces, I often remembered gratefully my rough, tough schooling in the Carpathian mountains.

The memory of Hulda was always with me. She had written from America and after I had seen an American postage stamp, touched a piece of paper that had actually been written there and had traveled all the way from New York to Riszka, the fabulous continent began to assume much more real proportions. Hulda had reassured me in her letter of her love. When, she asked, would I follow her? She wrote about the wonder city she was now living in: about houses as big as mountains, about trains traveling on giant bridges high above the city, about wonderful parades, about the big ships in the harbor. Every one of the things she was writing about defied my imagination. But her letters not only increased my longing for Hulda: they also began to fill me as I labored day after day in this Godforsaken corner of God's wonderful world with an absorbing longing to see for myself what was behind these mountains that seemed suddenly like prison walls. My thoughts by day and my dreams by night were filled with a mounting desire to set foot in the fairyland she was writing about, the land of plenty, the land of adventure and opportunity, the land that, if I could only get there, would give me everything I was longing for in life.

But it seemed a dream that could never become reality. Work went on relentlessly, day and night. Dave's and my salaries were collected by Father who, true to his iron principles of education and finance, allowed us only a crown per week. My only consolation was my violin. I played it on Sunday at the dances on the village green and, once in a while, with tired fingers and a desperate heart, after we had come home from one of our interminable fourteen-hour shifts. I had received one or two more letters from Hulda. But now she hadn't written for quite some time.

America, however, made another and quite unexpected entry into the monotonous life of the people of Riszka. A brilliant carriage stopped, one Sunday afternoon, in front of the General Store just when everybody was loafing around preparing for the usual afternoon dancing, drinking and stabbing. A stranger alighted. He was magnificently dressed. He wore a top hat, his boots sparkled brilliantly. He carried a walking stick with a golden handle. Nobody knew him, but a few minutes after he had entered the store we heard delighted screams from the inside. Within seconds the town knew that Moshe, the long-forgotten son of the Wasserbarts, had returned from America. He had left home almost twenty years before and nobody had ever heard from him again. Now he was back. His carriage was loaded with heavy trunks, and the trunks were loaded with magnificent gifts. His presence in the village—lasting only three days, he had to rush back to "his mansion in America"—was a general holiday. Not even Father had the power to make anybody work. After Moshe Wasserbart—or rather Maurice Waring as he called himself now—had left, everyone in the village felt even poorer than he had before. When Father handed me my weekly crown I went outside and cried.

Maurice had departed and the town was still talking and talking and talking about the prodigal son who had come home "an American millionaire"—anyone coming home as Moshe had done could be nothing less than a millionaire—when a letter arrived from Radautz, informing my parents that Grandma had passed away. The letter went on to say that Mother had inherited a third of the house. My father at once set out for Radautz to "settle matters."

It would never have occurred to Father to tell my mother or us or anybody else what he intended to do and it would never have occurred to my mother even to question him. The idea that Father could ever ask anybody's advice about anything was plainly unthinkable. After a few days he returned. He had sold Mother's share in the house for 900 kronen. He had the money with him, carefully stored in a money belt he had acquired for the occasion. He opened his shirt to let everybody touch the treasure that was tightly strapped to his body. There it rested, day and night.

For a man who had never had a bank account and who had, all his life, disposed of his meager income by paying up Mother's slips on the first of the month, the sudden presence of 900 kronen—equal to two and a half months of his salary—was an overwhelming experience. At once he began to plan what he was going to do with the money. He talked about trips to the city, about a wonderful tobacco he had seen at a *Specialitaeten Trafik,* about oranges—something quite fabulous in our parts, each one almost worth its weight in gold—about a new suit that would put to shame even the already legendary Maurice Waring.

But to me this sudden so utterly unexpected influx of wealth started a very different chain of thoughts. What had been unthinkable, forever outside of my reach—America—seemed suddenly within my grip! If I could muster the courage to approach the subject, to ask Father to give me a chance. . . . But nobody ever asked Father for anything. He did the thinking, he did the deciding in the famliy, in the mill, and in the town. The biggest thing I had ever asked for

was a five-gulden violin. But then, I had gotten my
wish, hadn't I? Maybe . . .

And so I kept on thinking, planning, wishing,
praying. The next days were a period of torment.
I knew that Father couldn't go back to town before
Sunday and thus I had a few days of grace. Then
came Saturday. The days of grace were gone. Tomorrow Father and with him "my" 900 kronen were
going back to Radautz and the treasure would go
up in oranges, suits and tobacco smoke. Without
thinking I shot up from my chair and said, as quietly
and modestly as I could manage:

"Papa. What about letting Dave and me go to
America?"

There was a sudden silence in the room. I could
see my mother pale and I still can see her lifting a
frightened hand to her mouth, as if she was trying
to make unsaid what she had just heard. The other
children didn't move. Father sat there, silent, rigid,
stunned.

By now a few of the things that I had repeated to
myself countless times during the last few days drifted
back to my mind.

"This is our chance," I said, pleading with growing
assurance, "our chance to invest this money in your
own future. If Dave and I go to America we will
make good, Papa. We will get jobs and make money
and then we will send for you and Mother and Jack
and Herman and Rose. Look what happened to
Moshe Wasserbart. It will happen to us and more so.
We won't miss, Papa, we just can't."

I stopped. I was too excited to say anything more. Everybody looked at Father, waiting for something terrible to happen. He still had not moved.

"I'll do it!" he suddenly snapped.

And when Father said he was going to do something everybody knew that he was going to do it. There was nothing else to be said.

The next few days things began to happen. Father decided that as long as Dave and I were going to America, Jack, two years our junior, might go as well. Now that he had made his decision he at once took complete charge of everything. He wrote to a friend of his in Czernowitz, the capital city of Bucovina, asking for advice on how to get transportation. The friend, a sewing-machine salesman by the name of Ehrlich (which means Honest—a name that, as we soon were to find out, did by no means fit its present bearer), wrote back to say that he would be happy to take care of everything, would Father just send the money and let him worry about the details. Father was delighted. His friend, he told us, was sure to give us the best possible service. And sure enough, a few weeks later the tickets arrived. We were to sail on the S.S. *Gerty*, in the words of honest Ehrlich "one of the finest passenger steamers in the transatlantic service." The size or nationality of the ship, the exact date of departure or the type of accommodation were not mentioned. All Mr. Ehrlich stated was that we must leave January 5, that we were to travel via Stanislav, Lemberg, Krakow, Vienna to Trieste, and that we would find the *Gerty* there waiting for us.

And so on January 5, in the forever unforgettable year of 1907, we two twins and Jack, newly equipped from head to foot, four valises, two straw baskets and four tremendous packages containing food—bread, apples, fried chicken, several jars of jelly and every other delicacy Mother had been able to think of, left our home for the railroad station. Father and Mother, two dogs and the two youngest children followed in a second carriage. At the last minute a Lithuanian laborer by the name of Kurek had joined us: he had saved some money and although he had no ship accommodation decided to trust his luck and to make the trip to Trieste with us, convinced that as long as he was holding on to Bernhard Winkler's three boys he couldn't fail to reach the distant land of his hopes.

Like all people who seldom travel we arrived at the station much too early. It was still one and one-half hours before the scheduled time of departure. No train was in sight and Father began to shout at once: we had disregarded his advice, had left much too late and had missed the train. When he inquired he was told that the train—Balkan railroads were completely oblivious of timetables—was four hours late. Everybody relaxed. It gave us a chance to talk things over, to review instructions, and it also made it possible for Mother to shed all her tears. After a few hours had passed, everybody was terribly tired. The tension created by the absence of the train and the impending separation of the family became unbearable. Even Mother stopped crying.

I sat on my valise in a feeling of deep bewilderment. This was the hour I had been waiting for. But where would that train, now due any moment, carry us? As I looked at my mother I felt that I had never realized how beautiful she was until this very moment. I suddenly felt an urge to get up and embrace her and to make good for all the heartaches and worries I had caused her. I wanted to promise her that I would from now on consider it my most holy obligation never to forget her and those she loved, and that I would make every effort to prove myself worthy of my new country and to do everything in my power to reunite our family. But I just sat there on my valise. I couldn't get up.

Then I looked at my father. He sat on one of the benches near the station house. Why wasn't he talking to us? Weren't we going away into a strange land, a land that none of us knew, away from home, away from him? He had been stern and his discipline had been unrelenting through all these years. But now as we were leaving I realized that he, too, loved us in his own, very personal way and had given us every chance to improve our station in life. But still, why didn't he speak to us?

Suddenly I saw him get up and walk over to where Dave and I were huddled on our bags. "Boys," he said, suddenly smiling the way I had never seen him smile, "I know that you have been stealing my tobacco for a long time and that you have rolled your cigarettes behind the house and up in the woods. I even saw you, Max, sitting on top of the pear tree and smoking one of my cigars."

We both got up in embarrassment. Was this the time for one of his famous sermons? What was he driving at?

He took two packages from the deep pockets of his topcoat.

"Here," he said. "I've bought each of you two packs of tobacco. Come on. Let's sit down and have a smoke together."

I shall never forget the light that shone in my mother's eyes when she saw her two oldest sons sit and smoke, like men, in the presence of their father. We all understood without anybody saying a word what Father wanted to say. We understood it and it made us proud and happy. Suddenly without warning there was a commotion at the end of the platform, people rushed out of the station house, calling frantically for their bags, their children, their wives, and the train pulled into the station. We four travelers grabbed our bags, parcels and baskets and started running like mad. Father, mother, sister and brother came running after us. We saw an open door, jumped in, tried to turn back once more for a word of good-by—but the door was slammed shut and before we could realize it we were off. I managed a last look at the little group as I squeezed myself through a mass of bags and legs to the little window. Then the train turned into a bend. They were gone. The great adventure had begun.

The three of us began to settle down. We traveled, of course, Third Class. To describe to anyone who all his life has traveled only on American railroads and whose lowest standard of traveling has been a trip by coach, on a nicely cushioned spotlessly clean seat that can be reclined at night, to describe to such a happily spoiled traveler what Third Class meant in an East-European train is well nigh impossible. The benches were of plain hard wood and so constructed that, if you tried to shape your forever aching spine to the back of it, the part of your body designed by nature to sit on was agonizingly suspended on a high curved board. If you slumped down, trying to sleep, it bored pitilessly into your back. If you changed your position to give your tormented bones a chance to rest, your neighbor would be aroused from an equally tortured slumber and push you back rudely. If you tried to stretch out, you kicked the man opposite who also tried to stretch out and could do so only by kicking back at you. At every curve a hail of valises, baskets and heavy sheep coats would come rumbling down on you.

The train was crowded. Soon the car was steaming hot. Nobody would ever open a window. The peasants, instead, began to take off their sheepskin coats, their boots, and the wet rags many of them had wrapped around their feet. All these wet clothes were hung up or piled around a red-hot wood-burning stove in a corner. The perfume of the steaming rags, the moist sheepskin vests, the sweating peasants, is still another item that I just cannot describe adequately to the lucky customers of the Pennsylvania or any other American railroad. Soon there were added the sharp smells of schnapps, of putrid goat

cheese, of pipes filled with the cheapest tobacco ever
to curl in heavy clouds around a tired prospective
emigrant boy's befuddled head. Twenty-four hours
after we had left, the doors were opened and the
sudden breeze of fresh air that swept into the car
almost made me faint. We were in Krakow, the
ancient capital of what had once been Poland, an
important railroad junction between the east, west
and south. Here we had to change trains. We collected our belongings and staggered out.

What we saw made us forget all our aches and
pains. The railroad station was a big magnificent
building with a huge glass dome covering a confusing combination of tracks. Every platform was
crowded with people, trains arriving and departing
in close succession—to us who had never seen anything bigger than the two-story houses of Radautz
and its one-track railroad station this was an overwhelming experience. It seemed like a first exciting
confirmation of what I had longed for—a first contact
with the big world beyond our mountains. Happily
I mingled with the crowds, watching the big loco-
motives, reading the signs on the trains that told of
fabulous destinations: Warsaw, Berlin, Vienna, Sofia,
Rome. It was late. Our little group timidly entered a
huge waiting room where we parked our bags in a
circle and settled down for the night. Our train for
Vienna and Trieste was not to leave until four o'clock
in the morning.

We were dead tired. The excitement of the last
few days—the suffocating trip, the last night spent on

that instrument of slow torture called a Third Class railroad bench, the exciting encounter with the first big town we had ever seen—all resulted in complete exhaustion. We just stretched out on the floor and fell immediately to sleep.

When I awoke heavily shaken by an impatient fist, I stared into a strange face, divided by a black Kaiser Franz Joseph beard and covered by a helmet whose shiny feathers identified its bearer even to my sleepy mind as one of His Majesty's gendarmes. At once I was wide awake. The big station clock was just approaching midnight. We had been sleeping not more than an hour.

A couple of other gendarmes had aroused Dave, Jack and Kurek. A man with a bigger and even blacker beard and with more feathers on his helmet was supervising the goings on.

"This one is David Winkler," one of the gendarmes reported to the supervising officer. He took Dave rudely by the wrist and shoved him towards the commanding officer.

Dave, trying to shake the sleep out of his heavy eyes, shivered with fright and confusion.

"Your name is David Winkler?" the officer repeated coldly.

"Yes, sir."

"Where are you going?"

"To America."

"Who are these other fellows?"

"My brothers and a friend, Kurek is his name, he . . ."

The officer didn't let him finish. "Take them all to headquarters," he said, turning around and disappearing in the crowd that had gathered around us. The gendarmes at once closed in. Curtly they commanded us to take up our baggage. One of them broke up the cordon of onlookers. The others, their bayonets pointed at their miserable prisoners, began to push us out of the waiting room and onto the street.

I don't know how long we marched. To me that procession through the dark streets of an unknown city, through snow and wind, seemed to last for hours. We were numb with confusion and staggered blindly, loaded with baggage, unable even to think. Every step took us farther away from the four o'clock train, from Trieste, from the S.S. *Gerty* waiting down there in a sunny harbor, from New York, from Hulda, from everything we had dreamed about.

At last we arrived at our destination. We were led into an office of tremendous proportions. The walls and the floors were stone. The doors were iron. The windows were barred. The light was cold and pale. All our belongings were taken from us. The guards told us to remove our suspenders and shoelaces and ties. Then one of the iron doors opened. Holding our trousers with one hand, clumsily shuffling along in unlaced shoes, we were pushed down a corridor. Another iron door opened. As it shut again the gendarmes had left. We were alone. I turned and tried the door. It was locked. We were standing there in complete darkness.

For a long time we stood, not daring to move, not daring to talk for fear that somebody might be in the room with us. Slowly our eyes began to penetrate the black pool of the night. We saw the faint contours of a barred window. There was nobody else in the cell, that much we could make out. But there were noises, an occasional rustle in the straw that was piled up in a corner. The noise was there even when none of us moved, even when we were holding our breath. None of us made that rustle. None of us moved. Who then did it?

At last we dared to move. We just fell down on the straw, unable to stand up any more. What had happened? we began to ask. None of us had even a guess. It seemed a terrible nightmare, something that just couldn't be—but all I had to do was listen to the clanking steps of the guard down in the courtyard and the reverberating echo to know that it was no nightmare but terrible reality. After a while I counted seventeen iron echoes to three seconds of silence. I counted again and again, seventeen steps, three seconds of silence, seventeen steps, three seconds of silence, the steps. the silence, the steps . . . Then I heard a train whistle in the distance. It pierced my heart. I was sure that this was our train, speeding south, to the ocean, to the gates of America—gone, gone forever.

The sun was high on the horizon the next day when a guard opened the door and commanded Dave to follow him. I tried to ask a question, to hold on to Dave, to prevent this first, terrifying separation, but

I was pushed back and the door again slammed shut. Hours must have passed before the guard came back. This time he called my name. I was led down a corridor. Through an open door I heard Dave's exhausted voice, crying in hysterics:

"I didn't do it. Please believe me. I didn't do it." Then they led me into another room. There were several desks and a number of clerks and gendarmes. Two important-looking men were obviously judges— or were they hangmen? I couldn't think any more.

One of them at once addressed me in a loud, terrifying tone.

"What's your name?"

"Max Winkler." I scarcely heard myself speak. One of the guards repeated the question in a low and friendly tone. I looked at him and felt moved by a deep gratitude. My voice came back.

"Do you have a brother?" the judge barked.

"I have three, Dave, Jack and Herman."

"How old are you?"

"I am five minutes less than Dave," I said.

"Less what?" thundered the judge.

I turned to face him and in trembling tones said:

"Dave was born on the fifteenth of March, 1888, and I was born five minutes later."

"Bring in the other fellow," the judge bellowed. A gendarme rushed out. A minute later he came back with Dave who was still crying hysterically. He stumbled forward and nearly fell into my arms when he saw me in the room. Everybody was staring at us.

The judge took up a piece of paper, glanced

through it and began a whispered conversation with the hangman next to him.

Suddenly he got up. "Send them back where they came from," he said.

An hour later we were back in the waiting room of the railroad station and as the 4 A.M. train for Vienna and Trieste finally pulled out of Krakow it had, I am sure, the happiest passengers on one of its Third Class benches that ever disregarded discomfort and aching spines with the unshakable conviction that nothing that fate might still have in store for them could ever equal the terrors of that past night. And only now, as I try to think about the incident as an American who knows about habeas corpus and the freedoms of a citizen, do I realize that never through this terrible experience did we question the right of these men to arrest, to torture us, to disrupt our lives, maybe beyond repair. Only now do I realize the difference between a *subject* and a *citizen*. As we traveled through the early morning we were only happy and relieved that it was all over. We still didn't question the right of the authorities just as we had never questioned the authority of our father.

In Vienna, where the train stopped for an hour, I bought a newspaper. And suddenly—I had never dreamed that our nightmare would be considered of interest to the readers of the imperial metropolis—my unbelieving eye was stopped by a headline. Excitedly I called my companions. This is what we read:

DAVID WINKLER STILL AT LARGE

David Winkler who on the 6th of October of last
year murdered Toreanu Ionescu and his wife in
Bucharest made a short appearance in police headquarters in Krakow yesterday only to be released
after a few hours of questioning. It turned out to
be the wrong David Winkler. During a routine
check in the Krakow railroad station a young man
by the name of David Winkler was apprehended.
However, after he produced an identical twin
brother the police had to let him go. Even the police
of Krakow knew that the real David Winkler has
neither a brother nor a sister. And so a killer is still
at large.

"Max," said Dave, suddenly trembling again as he
remembered the night of questioning, "I think you
have saved my life."

"Well," I said, proud and happy, "you saved me
from failing in geography—so none of us owes anything to the other."

We all had a good laugh. The train was moving
again. We passed the last chain of snow-covered
mountains. Then suddenly we traveled through valleys, green, sunny and beautiful—Here it was spring
while back home the icy winds blew through the
misty nights. We opened a window and let the glow-
ing sun shine on our faces. Suddenly Jack cried out,
"I see the ocean, I see the ocean!"

We all crowded around the window. There it was,
a motionless strip of water stretching through the
blue haze, endless, endless—all the way to America.

3.

In 1907, the United States had no quota. Immigrants were pouring in by the hundreds of thousands every year. If your eyes were free from trachoma, if your muscles could take a strong but friendly squeeze from an immigration inspector, if you were able to answer such routine questions as "What's your name?" "Where are you coming from?" "How old are you?"—if you were not deaf, dumb or blind, if you had two legs and two hands, if you answered "yes" to the question whether you had relatives in the United States and five dollars in your pocket (which both, relatives as well as dollars, you fortunately didn't have to show), you were permitted to enter the paradise of your hopes and dreams.

The *S.S. Gerty*, one of the many boats that transported the masses of eager but ignorant, poor and helpless people across the sea, had finally pushed her way up the bay, passed the Statue of Liberty, and was securely tied to some pier in Brooklyn. What a trip it had been! During the first few days of our voyage I could only smile when I remembered the letter in which Mr. Ehrlich, the supersalesman from Czernowitz, had advised us that he had been able to get passage for us "on one of the finest passenger steamers in the transatlantic service," and I wondered what my proud father would say should he ever hear how he had been taken in. The "finest passenger steamer" was a pitiful five-thousand-ton Italian cargo ship with steerage accommodations only. One of her rear holds had been rudely converted into a huge barrack where one hundred and twenty men, women, children, and babies slept on sixty upper and sixty lower cots. The walls of the room were of steel. The steel seemed continuously to sweat and water dripped from it day and night in tormenting monotony. The uppers and lowers were arranged in units of four; eight persons to a unit. They were divided by aisles just wide enough to permit one person to squeeze through. The room was wide open and one could see every bed.

Our section—we had managed through unrestrained application of physical force to stay together—was the first one near the only staircase that led up to the deck. My lower berth was about three feet from the landing of these stairs. This turned out to be a most unhappy arrangement. Several representatives of various units, bringing food (spaghetti with goulash sauce was the favorite dish) and drinks in open basins from the kitchen above, slipped at any hour of the day and night on these stairs and they as well as the contents of their dishes landed in my bed with enervating regularity.

The first day had been pleasant enough. To all these poor people the very fact that they were at last on a boat bound for America meant everything in the world: it meant a complete change in their lives and there was not a single man, woman or child on board who didn't look forward to the new life they were to begin, not with apprehension or fear but with excitement, assurance and hope. The overcrowded, filthy, dangerous ship, the disgusting food ladled out by the cooks in open trays that were never washed, the shocking sanitary facilities—all this meant nothing to them. At the end of the voyage, they knew, was the promised land. I, too, could only smile at the trick Mr. Ehrlich had played on Dad. What did it matter now? We were sailing through the blue, mild seas, away from the winter, away from Europe. Everybody was happy.

Soon various instruments began to appear, a flute, an accordion, a zither. Nobody played loudly. Every player seemed to play just for himself and his family or friends, trying to confine the expression of his happiness to his own little corner. But soon the noise grew stronger. First you only *saw* the mouth organs, the fiddles, the kazoos, the clarinets and trumpets— and then you began to *hear* them. As for myself and my fiddle, we had joined an old man who sang the familiar tunes of our own mountains with a strong voice that for a fleeting moment brought back the tender memories of my childhood and the beloved face of my mother to this hot, noisy, strange ship. I played—but soon I couldn't hear my own music any more. The room got hotter, the noise grew stronger. In the aisles that had looked too small for anybody to walk in, people began to dance.

They had come from all corners of Europe. They

spoke at least twelve different languages—and now they began to dance at least twelve different dances. There were polkas, waltzes, one-steps, tarantellas, kosatzkis, two-steps, mazurkas. Others sang their own folk tunes or the patriotic airs of their various countries—the very countries they were about to abandon forever. Still others could express their gratitude only in prayer and chant. Through all the stamping of feet, squeaking of instruments, crescendo of voices, mothers tried to pacify their children with gently rocking lullabies.

It was a terrifying symphony—but I am sure it sounded pleasing to the ears of the Lord. It was a symphony of thanksgiving, offered by these primitive people who knew no other way to express their feelings of redemption and hope. . . .

Yes, the first day had been pleasant enough. As the sun came up, more and more of the people climbed up the stairs to the one and only deck of the *Gerty*. It wasn't strictly what one would expect from "one of the finest passenger steamers in the transatlantic service." It was flanked, on each end, by the community washrooms and toilets. In the middle of the deck were the kitchen facilities. And to add further beauty to the picture, behind the kitchen were about twenty live cows and steers with plenty of hay. Cargo ships in those days had no refrigeration. Meat was carried on the hoof and knocked off when it was needed. The part of the deck not occupied by toilets, kitchen refuse or cows and their dung was left to the passengers. There were no chairs or benches, of course. But you could always sit down on the deck (if you found any space, that is) and enjoy the air and the sunshine. The sea was calm.

But that was only one day—the first day of a voyage that was to last thirty-five days and thirty-five nights! I don't want to remember many of these days; the days when the happy crowd of grateful travelers was aroused by fights that only half a dozen sailors with all the brutal force of sailors could quell. The days, many of them, when women cried for help for a sick child—and no doctor or any other medical facilities on board. The day when we woke up to find a sky filled with dark clouds and watched the sailors fasten ropes all over the deck.

All day the wind was howling, the waves grew bigger. It started to rain. The ropes and ladders began singing a weird song. Everybody was ordered inside. Every window, the door and every porthole were closed tight. Many of the one hundred and twenty people locked in the room without air became violently sick.

But still the storm grew in intensity. It seemed as if the ship were going up a mountain, falling down— roll right, roll left, go straight for about two or three seconds, and then go up the mountain again. The mountains seemed higher every time, and the valleys deeper. The ship was trembling and moaning as if in pain.

The people, helplessly locked in the room that became unbearably hot, started praying. Some were kneeling in the aisles, others prostrated themselves on their cots. I have never seen nor heard so many different ways of imploring the Lord for help. Some expressed their prayers in song, some tried to dance, some bowed, some knelt, some prayed facing north, some south. Some kissed the floor of the ship in a supreme gesture of submission. Women and men and children cried for help. Many of them were so sick that they prayed to their God for deliverance through death.

But I don't want to remember the storm, the fights, the sickness, the people who died and were buried at sea, the growing nervousness and hostility of the travelers as the prisonlike routine of the endless voyage began to tell. What I want to remember is the day, February 19, 1907, when we first saw a coast that we knew was the coast of America and then, later, the symbol of our new country, huge, strong, towering: the Statue of Liberty. Many, again, fell on their knees. Everybody was on deck, and the deck was rocking in ever-growing waves of laughter, tears, embraces, kisses and dances. It was a riot of brotherhood. Nothing that had happened to us in the past mattered any more. And as the Manhattan skyline revealed itself in its unmatched greatness before our astonished and unbelieving eyes something even stranger happened. We all stopped dancing, laughing, crying and kissing. We just froze. We stood and looked and looked, speechless, motionless, wondering that this tremendous mass did not sink into the ocean.

This is the day and the hour I like to remember.

And, later, the docking of the ship, the immigration officers coming on board and pinning large identification cards on our chests. The tender that took us over to Ellis Island, the final gateway to the land of our dreams. The tender was terribly crowded. It was windy and cold and as we were in the middle of the upper bay snow began to fall.

An hour later, after having gone through a fast and not too thorough interrogation and a much faster and much more thorough delousing process, we were given a wonderful meal. Uncle Sam was the host and I am sure that none of his grateful guests will ever forget their first American dinner—the first ham and eggs, the first apple pie, the mountains of white bread. Then—it was about three in the afternoon by now—a barge landed the four of us at the foot of the Battery. We took our bags and stepped ashore. Our journey was over.

We found a bench in Battery Park, wiped off the snow and sat down. There before my eyes was the tremendous city, bigger, noisier, more terrifying in its dimensions than any of us had ever been able even to imagine. How were we ever to become a part of this forbidding, strange world—how would we ever be at home among these people we saw rushing around on unknown errands, speaking a language we didn't know, having lived all their lives in dimensions that terrified us? Never before had I felt so alone.

I am sure we all four felt the same. But here **we** were—there was no way back. We had to look for-

ward. First we began counting our cash. We three
Winkler boys had exactly $12.18 between us—the
leftover from the hundred kronen Father had given
us as we left home. And then we had the address of
Aunt Minnie, my father's sister. She was living at
115 St. Mark's Place. But how to find her, how to
get there? Whom to ask and how? People were hurry-
ing past us all the time—but nobody ever stopped
and when we approached one or two of them they
seemed to accelerate their steps. Suddenly a policeman stopped at our bench, swinging a stick. We got
up in terror, all four of us. All our lives we had known
that a policeman could only mean trouble. It was
probably *verboten* to sit on a bench or to park valises
on the grass or to approach strangers. Something,
surely, was *verboten* and here was the law to en-
force it.

"Where you fellows want to go?" the policeman
asked us in German.

I was overwhelmed. What a wonderful question.
How did he know that we didn't know where to go?
How did he know that we didn't speak English?

I took out my little black book and showed him
Aunt Minnie's address.

"That's a long way from here. You fellows got
twenty cents?"

"*Ja, ja, ja!*" we answered in rapid succession.

"Come on—I'll show you."

We took our valises and as he led us through the
snow-covered park I couldn't help thinking back to
that last police-escorted march in Europe—through

the snow-covered streets of Krakow. What a farewell from the old continent—and what a welcome in the new one! The policeman led us up some stairs to a railroad station. "Get on the first train going in that direction," he said, pointing forward. "I'll tell the guard to let you off on 8th Street. Walk down the steps to the street. People will show you where St. Mark's Place is. Just ask anybody—and don't be afraid," he added, as if he were reading our troubled minds.

The train came roaring into the station. "Good-by, boys," we heard him say as we scrambled to the doors, "and good luck to you!"

Aunt Minnie welcomed us with open arms. She was a widow, living with three young, unmarried daughters on the fourth floor of a five-story tenement house, a stone's throw from Avenue A. A letter from our parents was awaiting us. It had outspeeded—easily enough, I am sure—the *S.S. Gerty* and was a touching and unexpected welcome in the new world. We read it eagerly and then we got a wonderful meal. Neighbors drifted in. We sat and ate and talked until midnight. Then Aunt Minnie escorted us upstairs where she had found a room for us. For $4.50 a week we had a bed for two and a small sofa for one and a cup of coffee and two rolls in the morning. A woman whose face I couldn't see in the dark admitted us and led the way through several dark rooms, heavy with the breath of sleepers. She closed the door behind us. We undressed and went to bed.

I couldn't fall asleep. I lay there, my hands folded under my head. Faint noises from the street seeped through the window—the clatter of hoofs on the pavement, cries, drunken bits of songs, a police whistle, the distant clang of a fire engine. So this is my first night in America, I thought. This is the culmination of my hopes and dreams. Here I am, in a strange land, penniless, without my friends, without my father and mother. I have one suit of clothes with two buttons missing on the vest, an overcoat, one pair of shoes, three shirts—two clean and torn, one dirty and good. Why did I ever come here? What made me do it? How am I going to survive?

Dave next to me slept deep and peacefully. I didn't dare to move. I just kept on staring into the dark till, at last, I drifted away. . . .

But in the morning the sun broke brightly through our little window. The house was already shaking with activity. We got up, refreshed, eager, ready to dive head-on into our new lives. Next to our little room—only now when we saw it for the first time we realized just *how* little it was for three big fellows— was the "dining room"—the sleeping quarters for three of the older children. Next was "the bedroom." Here our landlady and her husband slept on one side of a dirty curtain strung up on a rusty piece of wire, and three small children slept on the other side. Whenever a child left the tender age of innocence, he was, it seemed, removed to the dining room. From the bedroom you would step into the kitchen and then, at the very end of this succession of chambers, reach the bathroom where one cold-water sink and one toilet served the needs and habits of all eleven inhabitants.

Well, we emerged at last and walked down the stairs and out on the street. For the first time we were carrying no valises. For the first time we had to think about something else but traveling, passports, trains. America, suddenly, had become a reality. It wasn't our problem any more how to get here. A much more serious one had arisen—what to do to stay here alive. We had to find work and fast.

On the stairs leading up to the house—called "the stoop"—we found already at this matinal hour an odd assembly of people, talking, sitting around, watching the traffic on the street, setting out to or returning from shopping. We newcomers were at once the object of concentrated curiosity. Jokes were made at our expense, particularly by those who had arrived on these shores only a few weeks ahead of us and couldn't pour enough fun on the greenhorns. Soon, however, the conversation narrowed down to the one and only topic that concerned us at this critical hour: how to go about getting a job.

It was Mr. Wolf, a German who had come to St. Mark's Place and, for that matter, to America only a few months before, who took a particularly determined and flattering interest in our affairs. "Let's go to the candy store, *meine Herren,*" he urged us at last. "Will you please give me the pleasure to be my guests for a round of cherry sodas and pretzels?" So we sat around a little marble table, sipping our

first American refreshments, and Wolf told us about
the people living here and about people living in
Manhattan, about downtown and uptown, about
trains and buses, about politics and dance halls, about
where to take a girl and where to bet on horses—and
we just sat, dumb, openmouthed, wondering and
marveling. At last he produced a copy of the *Staatszeitung,* the biggest newspaper we had ever seen.
"This is where you will find your jobs," he said, pointing out a seemingly endless list of classified ads. It
looked simple enough. All we had to do was go and
pick a job. Our spirits lifted. We took the paper and
got up.

Wolf, who somehow seemed to take me for the
chosen leader of our little group, discreetly pulled
me into a corner. "I am most embarrassed to find
myself without funds today," he whispered. "Would
you mind paying for the cherry sodas? This means,
of course, I owe you eight cents—*Ehrenwort.*" And
he took out a little black book and in a meticulous,
very German hand put down the debt and the date.
In the weeks and months to come Wolf "invited"
me almost daily for a cherry soda or an occasional
cup of coffee. He was always out of funds but he
always put down the amount in his little book. After
we had indulged up to the amount of $5.67 he dis-
appeared one day and never came back. He remains
in my memory as one of the many teachers to whom
I owe eternal gratitude for a practical course in the
rudiments of life in America. . . .

Dave, Jack and I walked down the street together,

each of us with a section from the *Staatszeitung*
tightly clutched in his hand. At the corner we parted.
Suddenly, at this very moment, we had ceased to be
three boys. We were three men—stepping out into
the big city, stepping out into life, into the unknown
life whose very course might be decided in the hours
to come. Kurek, companion of our travels, had already left us and set out on a life of his own: he was
going to Massachusetts, to work on the chicken farm
of some Lithuanian relatives. I never heard from him
again.

When I came home that night tired, exhausted,
hungry, and climbed up the stairs to our little room
I had learned one or two things. I had learned that
the United States was going through a "money
panic." I didn't know what a money panic was but I
had found out that there were hundreds and thousands who, like me, were guided through the streets
of New York by a clipping from a newspaper, mark-
ing off job after job as they were turned down and,
finally, reaching in despair the last of these classified
ads that had looked so promising in the morning and
looked so depressing and disappointing at night. I
had waited in front of a hardware store as No. 26 in
line for a job that was given, not to No. 1 but to
No. 17 after the man had walked up and down the
line, looking over the men like cattle and then picking one who seemed to be suited for the job. When
I reached the second place, a grocery store, the line
was even longer. The third place, after walking for

an hour, I couldn't find. As I arrived at the fourth there was a sign "Job filled." By now it was late, too late to continue. I looked up. I was on 37th Street and Sixth Avenue. Night began to fall. I walked and walked and walked.

When I came home Dave was already in bed. He was too excited to sleep. He had been waiting for me —he had to tell me. He had a job! He was to be the assistant to a man who peddled coffee, sugar and tea from house to house. He had already worked a few hours today and he was to start again tomorrow morning at five. His job was to watch the horse and wagon while the man went about his business. He was to work twelve hours a day, six days a week and his salary was to be six dollars.

But where was Jack? Little Jack, too, had gone out in the morning. But now it was late—and no sign, no word from him. Why had I let him go alone? Hadn't I promised Father to take care of him, to keep the family together till we were all united again? What could I do? Where to look for him out in the vastness of this terrifying city? Again the noises from the street, the cries and songs, the uneasy moaning of the sleepers in the next room. Again no sleep. Where was Jack? What was I going to do?

The next morning there was a letter from Jack, hastily written with pencil. He had met a fellow who had told him that the Erie Railroad was looking for mechanics. The man had taken him down to the water front and Jack had signed up then and there and had just time to mail the letter—he was to leave immediately for Port Jervis, N. Y. By now he was there already—working in a job, and just the thing he was made for. He had always been an amateur mechanic. I was happy. But when I told Aunt Minnie she cried out.

"Mein Gott," she said, "don't you know the Erie Railroad has a strike on—they are hiring strike break-ers—there has been shooting and riots. Port Jervis— Here, look for yourself." And she handed me the *Volkszeitung*—there were three German dailies in New York at that time—with a report on the violence in Port Jervis! But Jack was gone—nothing could bring him back. I tried to get him off my troubled mind and went again on my endless errands through New York. Again I failed.

The next morning I was in line in front of a shoe store at 4:30. When the man opened his door at nine a long line of men had formed down the block. He came out and looked at me. I was, at last, No. 1. My heart was beating heavily.

"You're too big for the job," the man said. "I want a boy, not a man."

He turned.

"But, mister," I tried to plead, "mister, look here . . ."

"Beat it!" he said. "Beat it!"

And again I walked through the streets. I passed through the wide streets of midtown Manhattan and through the crowded, dirty, narrow streets of my East Side. I saw pushcarts, hundreds of them, loaded with fruits and vegetables. I saw stores filled with delicacies. I saw barrels and boxes filled with refuse and in many of the boxes I saw big pieces of bread. A big piece, half a loaf almost, had fallen off a barrel and was lying there in the mud. I was shocked to the depths of my heart. How could anyone throw away bread? A man passed by and carelessly kicked the loaf of bread from the sidewalk into the street.

I had been taught that bread was holy. If we dropped a piece of bread at home we would pick it up quickly, say a prayer and kiss it. Here, people walked on bread. And I was hungry. Others kicked bread in the dirt and I was hungry. . . .

The next day I didn't wait in line any more. I walked through the streets determined to find a job by just asking for one. Dave and the coffee salesman weren't waiting till people asked them in. They knocked at the doors if they wanted a new customer.

And so, before the day was over, I had made my first twenty-five cents! I had noticed two men dragging an unpainted wooden wardrobe out of a cellar. I stopped and looked down a steep stairway.

"Need any help?" I asked.

"Sure," one of the men replied. "Push that corner over there. The darn thing is stuck in the wall."

I put my shoulder to the wardrobe, pushed, and practically lifted it out to the sidewalk.

"You're strong. Where you from?" asked one of the men. He already addressed me in German.

"I'm from Bucovina," I replied. "Just got here about a week ago. I am looking for a job. Got one?"

The man looked me over.

"Know something about this business?" he said at last.

"Sure."

"Can you varnish a wardrobe or a door?"

"Sure, I can." Pausing for a second, I continued, "Just show me. They do things different in America."

I didn't have the slightest idea how to varnish anything. But how would I ever learn, I reasoned, unless I tried?

"All right, come downstairs. I'll give you a try, for twenty-five cents an hour."

The carpenter took out a cabinet door that was to be varnished. He showed me some brushes, varnish, sandpaper, rags and tools. "Go ahead," he said, "start working."

"Show me," I said. "We do this kind of work different where I come from. I want to do it your way."

"All right," said the carpenter. "Watch me."

His demonstration lasted about five minutes.

"Now you start working. We got to deliver the closet. If somebody should come in, just call my wife. She's back in the kitchen."

They left and I was alone with my brushes, my cabinet door, my varnish, my rags, and my ignorance. No matter how I tried to follow the carpenter's instructions, something always went wrong. By the time the carpenter came back, the door was an awful sight. "Holy Hell!" he roared. "You crazy fool! You've ruined that door! What the hell kind of a varnisher are you? Get out of here, or I will murder you."

"Now wait a minute," I tried to plead. "Give me a chance. The job isn't finished."

"Whaaat? Not finished yet? Don't you touch that door again."

"All right," I told him, "I worked an hour and a half. I'll settle for one hour. Give me my twenty-five cents."

By now, the carpenter was wild. He was spinning like a top. He grabbed a hammer, he lurched towards me and shouted, "Get out, you bum, or I'll split your head!"

I saw red. I knocked the hammer out of his hand, grabbed him by his coat lapels, and lifted him several feet into the air. My old wrestling tactics came in very handy. At this moment the carpenter's wife came out of the kitchen screaming, "Give him the twenty-five cents. You never know what kind of thieves and robbers walk the streets these days. Give him the money before he kills us all!"

She shot up the stairs like a bolt of lightning and returned with a quarter. Before the carpenter could catch his breath she had kicked me up the stairs, handed me the money and slammed the door in my bewildered face. "Herman, stay here—the bum will murder you!" were the last words I heard her exclaim as I turned and walked down the street.

During the next few days I made fifty cents by unloading furniture from two in the afternoon to ten-thirty at night and seventy-five cents by washing half a dozen horses in a stable on 23rd Street. Dave paid the rent. Aunt Minnie kept on feeding me on credit. With the quarter the carpenter's wife had given me—I had some misgivings about the way it had been earned and felt that the money should be invested in something that would make atonement for my deed—I had bought an English-German dictionary and while I was waiting in futile lines or resting once in a while on a park bench I began to learn more and more words, hundreds of them. Soon I asked my landlady and Aunt Minnie to talk only English to me.

I felt deeply discouraged by now. Dave worked and Jack wrote from Port Jervis where the strike had been settled that he was doing fine and staying on the job and making fourteen dollars a week. It sounded like a fortune to me. I just had no luck.

And then, one morning, I heard music. I was just ready to leave on one of my daily rounds when I saw an odd assortment of men assembled in the backyard. There was a trumpet, a tuba, an accordion, a clarinet and a bull fiddle. There they stood, playing underneath the wash that was swinging in the morning breeze, their unshaved dirty faces lifted towards the fire escapes. Suddenly I had a thought. I rushed back upstairs and took my fiddle out of the case where it had been sleeping in silence since we had left the boat. I went down and began to play. In the windows I saw faces, and children appeared on the fire escapes, among the boxes and pots. Soon a few pennies began flying down. The man with the bull fiddle stopped playing and began to collect the money. Then they all bowed and filed out to the street.

I followed them. But the man with the bull fiddle turned around and when he spoke his voice was as wild and threatening as I had never heard a voice before.

"If you ever try again to mix yourself up in my business," he hissed, "I'll kill you, you dirty son of a bitch!"

I walked back to the house. I put my fiddle back in the case. I sat down and took off my hat. I was dead tired and unhappy beyond description. But there was something sticking in the brim of my hat. Almost mechanically I pulled it out. It was a penny, dark and flat with age. I polished it carefully and put it in a pocket close to my heart. Suddenly I felt myself smile in confidence. Suddenly I knew that I was still going to lick that city and that somewhere there was to be a place for me. I felt happy, strong and sure.

As I left the house, a little later, friend Wolf was sitting on the stoop.

"Come on," he said when he saw me come down the stairs. "Come on, I'll buy you a soda."

"I am sorry." I smiled. "I don't think I can afford it today."

Wolf took it good-heartedly.

"Sit down here with me," he said. "What's your hurry?"

What really was my hurry? Pennies were raining

down on me out of the open sky. I had no reason
in the world to worry. I sat down in the sunshine.

"So you are playing the fiddle," Wolf took up the
talk. "A fiddler, hm, a musician."

He unfolded the *Staatszeitung*. "Here is something
for you, Maestro. What about trying, *wunderkind?*"

I took the paper. It said that a music publishing
house was looking for a boy and to apply in writing,
Box 65, *Staatszeitung*.

I walked over to the candy store and took out my
penny. "You'll bring me luck," I heard myself say.
"I know it, you'll bring me luck." The woman behind
the counter looked at me queerly. I handed her the
penny.

"Give me a stamp—I have to write a letter."

"You can't write a letter for a penny," she said.

Then she must have seen my sagging, disappointed
face. "Here—I give you a postcard for your penny."

I took it and walked over to the little marble table.
I thought for a long time. Then I put down the best
words I knew, beginning with a solemn *Sir* and ending with a *Respectfully yours* and in between trying
to explain that I played a violin and was a musician
and would take any, underlined any, job. I addressed
it carefully. Box 65. No waiting in line this time.
No boss picking the next man because you were too
tall or too young or too old. Box 65. A shiny office
somewhere, a music publisher surrounded by stacks
of music: "Here is an application from a young man
who plays the violin, a musician, just the man we
need. Miss Crawford, take a letter to Max Winkler,

Fifth Floor, 115 St. Mark's Place—Dear Sir, we are in receipt of and we will be delighted to . . ."

I walked over to the corner and slowly saw the postcard slide down in the mailbox. Then I went home. I didn't go out for the rest of the day. For the first time since I had come to America I just lay on my bed, dreaming and thinking and smiling. When Dave came home he found me stretched out there, fully dressed and sleeping peacefully.

4.

Three days passed. Three days of waiting for the mailman, of seeing him pass the house on his dreary rounds and disappear around the corner towards Avenue A. I couldn't get myself to leave the house in a paralyzing fear that a message might arrive, and that I might miss the appointed hour to meet my unknown boss—the man who began to take on in my excited mind the appearance of a mystical benefactor. I could see him, looking like the good Lord I had once seen on an early picture of the Creation—a long beard, a benevolent smile—a fatherly protector who would take me out of my misery and make me a useful citizen of my new country.

Dave began to get irritated when he came home at night and saw me loafing around the house. Aunt Minnie didn't say anything. She still fed me on credit, but it wasn't difficult to feel that she began to wonder just how long this big lug was still going to sit on her pocket.

But I didn't move. Ever since I had mailed that postcard I was filled with a childish confidence that here, here alone was going to be my salvation. I read for hours in my little dictionary. In Aunt Minnie's meager library I had found a little booklet, "How to Become an American Citizen." Here I made my first acquaintance with the great principles of the American creed. I read the Constitution of the United States and its amendments, I read and tried to memorize the words of "The Star Spangled Banner," I explored the basic facts of the history and philosophy of my new country—and began, for the first time, fully to understand what it meant to be an American. It would be five more years before I would be eligible to be a citizen, I read—and it looked like a very long time. But then, as I kept on reading about the government of the people, by the people, for the people, as I began to understand the fundamental thoughts of the Constitution and the tremendous accomplishments of the history of this country, I was filled with a deep and ever-growing conviction that only the Lord could have done a better job than the framers of these laws and that a five-year probation period wasn't too long for anybody to prove himself worthy of the privileges of citizenship and the final and unreserved admittance to the land of freedom, justice and liberty.

I don't know how many times I read the little book over and over again during these days of voluntary house arrest. When I got tired I just lay on my bed, staring at the ceiling and waiting for the next round of the postman which would find me sitting on the stoop, looking down the street till I would see the already familiar figure approach—and pass. Once in a while, to kill the time, I took out my little black book. There, right on the first page and framed with large red pencil—the intense color of love—was the

name of Hulda and the American address of her
people—46 Avenue B. It was only a few blocks from
where Aunt Minnie lived. My heart went out to her;
but when I looked at the appearance of my pants and
shoes and counted the contents of my pockets—no
contents at all—I decided that Hulda, as everything
else in my life, just had to wait for the arrival of that
letter. I put the little black book back in my pocket
and Hulda's picture out of my mind and went down
to take my observation post on the stoop. Wolf was
there. He joined me in silent watch.

And then the mailman came and the mailman
stopped and the mailman came up the stairs.

"Does a Max Winkler live here?" the mailman
said. That was all. No flags, no cannon firing a
salute, no drums and trumpets and fanfares. Just a
mailman asking whether Max Winkler was living
here. And a mailman handing me a letter. The flags
were in my heart and the whole street was echoing
with the drums of victory and the trumpet of redemption.

It was Friday morning, March 15—and suddenly
I remembered that it was my birthday. I was nineteen years old. I took the letter, sat down again on the
stoop and opened it. It was a very short letter and,
as I remember it today, contained only a single
sentence. But I read it again and again. Then I
handed it to Wolf. I wanted to make sure that I had
understood every word of it. After all, it was the
first English letter I had ever received. Yes, I was

right. The letter came from Carl Fischer, Music Publishers, Cooper Square, and requested that I present myself as soon as possible—*"so bald als moeglich,"* Wolf repeated triumphantly. He had, after all, instigated the idea and felt himself already my sponsor in the big world of commerce.

The Carl Fischer Music House was a combination of five four-story brick buildings—only two and a half blocks from where I lived! Many times, almost every day when I set out on my wanderings, I had stopped there to look at the shiny instruments, the beautifully displayed music, the busts of great composers in the windows. The big clock of the Cooper Union building was striking noon when I stood again before these windows. I was trembling. I had to stop and wait till my heart stopped pounding. Then I walked through the door.

The store at once enveloped me with its heavy atmosphere of old paper and old furniture. The room I was looking into was about eighteen feet wide—but there were doors leading to other departments. To my left an old man was sorting out strings. Once in a while when a customer approached his counter he turned around and whistled in the mouthpiece of a brass tube. At once, through the tube, came an acknowledgment—I was sure it sounded like *Was willst Du*—and then the old man mumbled something in the tube. I watched him with fascination—I had never seen a gadget like this. "Bring down them strings—cuschtomer waiting," I heard him say with a heavy Teutonic accent, and as if by magic a few moments later a boy arrived and the old man handed the "cuschtomer" whatever he had wanted. No jet plane nor the marvels of the atomic age have ever impressed me more and convinced me as decisively of the superiority of American streamlined life as old man Roemhild and his magic tube.

The walls of the store, all the way up to the ceiling, were covered with shelves—and in the shelves I saw neatly labeled boxes, hundreds of them. Big signs explained that they contained piano, vocal and violin music; and narrow wooden ladders, creakingly moving on steel rails, were constantly occupied by clerks climbing up like monkeys and coming down, balancing one or several boxes with elegant assurance. In the middle of the room was a cashier's box with high iron bars. The place had a few windows but even at this hour of the day the gas lamps were burning and there was a sizzling sound, a constant never-ceasing hissing that seemed to drip down from the lights on everything and everybody in hypnotizing monotony.

Nobody seemed to notice me. One or two of the clerks looked at me with some uneasiness—it was obvious that I didn't impress them as the type of customer they were used to seeing in the place. At last I stopped one of the boys who had just unloaded a huge stack of music on one of the counters and handed him my letter. He glanced at it, took it and disappeared.

Twenty minutes—I could see the hands of the big clock moving—ticked away. Then, suddenly, I saw a short stocky man with a well-groomed beard cross through the store and walk briskly towards me. He stopped very close to me and looked at me silently.

"Are you Max Winkler?" he asked at last. His voice sounded angry and impatient.

"*Jawohl,*" I said trembling, forgetting where I was.

The man didn't seem to mind. "I am glad you came," he said in a flawless, very Prussian German. "I just wanted to see the fellow who had the audacity to apply for a position on a postcard."

Then he turned and briskly walked away.

I felt an explosion in my head.

"Just a minute!" I shouted—and I saw the clerks turn behind their counters, the boys stop in their busy errands, customers get up from their stools. But I also saw the bearded gentleman stop as if frozen in his tracks. He turned around—and I have never before or after seen a more flabbergasted face. His face behind the black beard looked white.

I made a few steps and was now near him. I looked down on him—he was small and fat—and he seemed still paralyzed by surprise.

"You didn't give me a chance to answer," I said, keeping my voice down and talking with the intensity of desperation.

"What answer"—he stammered—"what do you want?"

"I just wanted to tell you why I applied for this job on a postcard," I said, suddenly very calm. "It's really very simple, mister. I had only one penny—and a letter needs two."

He retreated a few steps. The clerks had resumed their ministrations, the boys were rushing again, the customers had settled down to their business. The man with the beard looked at me again—and when he spoke his voice sounded slightly changed. It wasn't subzero any more—just around zero, maybe a little above.

"Is that the truth?" he said.

"It certainly is," I asserted, and my voice must have sounded as convincing as if I had sworn a solemn oath.

"We can't use you anyway," he said, moving again. "We advertised for a boy, not for a man."

I kept going with him. "A man can do the work of a boy," I said, suddenly determined not to let go, to succeed, to hold on to this one chance till they threw me out bodily. "I have pushed wardrobes up cellar stairs and washed horses and dug ditches—but I want to work here. I want to work in a music house. Give me a chance, mister."

"Are you willing to work for the salary of a boy?" he suddenly asked.

"I'll work for any salary—"

"Come in Monday. I'll give you a job."

"I can't wait till Monday."

For a moment I thought he would again break out in a flare at the *unverschaemte Kerl*—but he just turned and asked one of the boys to get Mr. Hoffmann. Within an instant Mr. Hoffmann arrived, breathlessly.

"This is your new boy," the man with the beard

said. "He can start right away. We'll pay him six dollars."

Then he walked away. Hoffmann didn't say a word. He just looked at me, then shrugged his shoulders as if to express his supreme contempt for a man who hired people like me, and walked away. I followed him down a squeaky wooden stairs into the cellar.

Hoffmann kept on going. He speedily wormed his way through a labyrinth of shelves that seemed to fill every square inch of the basement. He knew of course every turn of the tricky passage, every protruding package of music, every connecting steel beam—but I didn't. I bumped against sharp edges, I hit my head that was at least a foot or two too high for the dimensions of this place—but I kept on following my taciturn guide. From this very minute on and for a long time to come I was possessed by an agonizing fear of losing my job. And so I kept rushing after the elusive Hoffmann—through one, two, three rooms that all seemed alike, all filled to the rafters with music and dust, all smelling heavily, filled with a foul air and poorly lighted by a few gaslights or an isolated kerosene lantern. At last I saw light: it was like the opening in a forest, and presently we entered a room where I saw four or five men sorting out music sheets on large wooden tables. In a corner was a rolltop desk, covered with immense books. Hoffmann sat down behind the desk, called over a man by the name of Goetz—the loudest beer-bellied German it has ever been my misfortune to meet—and asked him to put me to work.

Goetz took a long look at me, turned around and led the way back to from where we had come. This time the trip was less dangerous: Goetz had too much trouble squeezing himself through the passages and around the corners. At last he stopped in a niche. There was a small table, a lamp hanging down from the ceiling, an inkwell and some paper on the table.

Goetz pointed to a stack of music. "Put down every copy of this song," he said. "We have to make an accounting to the composer. Don't make a mistake, *bloeder Kerl*—get going." And he left. I took the first stack of songs, broke open the wrapper and began to work feverishly.

Once in a while, like ghosts, I saw the dimly lit figures of men rushing through the narrow aisles, taking out some music from one of the racks or bringing new mountains of packages down the stairs. Otherwise the place was quiet. The air was heavy with dust and the smell of decay. The light was poor. I never paused in my work.

I didn't know how much time had passed when Hoffmann suddenly appeared through one of the aisles. "What is the matter with you, *Dummkopf*—can't you count a few thousand copies of a lousy song in an afternoon?"

Then he stopped. I saw his face go dark. And then he broke out in a cascade of roaring, hysterical laughter. It lasted for minutes. He slapped me on the back, unable to control himself. Then Goetz squeezed his mighty body through aisle No. 483.

"Look here," I heard Hoffmann moan, "if this isn't the funniest . . ."

I didn't know what was so funny. I had sat in this hole, for hours and hours, without air and drink and food—and there I had almost forty sheets of paper before me, every one of them neatly covered in my best and most careful handwriting:

1. Your Lovely Eyes Smile at Me
2. Your Lovely Eyes Smile at Me
3. Your Lovely Eyes Smile at Me
4. Your Lovely Eyes Smile at Me
5. Your Lovely Eyes Smile at Me. . . .

By the time I was so rudely interrupted by Hoffmann I had just put down, at the bottom of page 40:

2763. Your Lovely Eyes Smile at Me

I had only a few hundred more to go. . . .
This was my first day in the music business.

A week later, however, I had become a full-fledged member of the basement brigade.

I had survived a succession of days filled to the brim with ridicule and abuse. Several of my co-workers expressed their appreciation of the new-comer by holding their nostrils every time I passed them. Hoffmann and Goetz made me work till, at night, I could scarcely drag myself up the cellar stairs. I moved heavy tables, I swept endless floors, I counted thousands of copies of music and put them back on the racks—and when someone had to clean the toilets it was "the slimy Polack" who was designated for the job.

On Wednesday truckload after truckload of music arrived in front of the house. Fischer's had bought the catalogue and complete stock of a music publisher in Philadelphia who was going out of business. There were hundreds and thousands of titles—not one of them worth even the price of transportation from Philadelphia to New York. But among all this senseless mess of pieces for zither, mandolin and string ensembles were a few of John Philip Sousa's most celebrated marches—"Washington Post," "Semper Fidelis," "The Thunderer"—and the presence of these few pearls in that huge pile of junk amply made up for the deal. Here, if I had known anything about it, I could have had my first free lesson in the secrets and ramifications of the music publishing business; but all I knew then was that Mr. Hoffmann took one look at these trucks, waiting out there in snow and ice, and already had me selected for the job to unload them and carry them—the music was wrapped in packs weighing 150 to 200 pounds each—to a storeroom on the fifth floor of an adjoining building.

By four o'clock in the afternoon two hundred of these packages were in their racks. Before they had been loaded on the trucks they must have been stored, for years undoubtedly, in a windowless basement. They were covered with the finest powdered dust that could filter into your lungs and make you cough blood after you had breathed it—making two hundred trips to the fifth floor—for a couple of hours. I stuck my head under a faucet to stop it from hammering itself off my neck. Just then Hoffmann passed by.

"You dirty peasant," he yelled, "are you used to this kind of comfort from where you come from? Get going—if you don't finish the job by night you are fired."

Again that panicky fear of losing my job—a job that so far had only brought me humiliation and unbearable toil—made me turn in silence and continue my work. What made me do it? I don't know. But I had made up my mind to stick it through—as long as anyone could stick it through. And strangely enough, my method began to work. The insults and attacks slowly began to stop. Somebody had given me the nickname "Jumbo," and I didn't mind it. I looked it up in my dictionary—"anything of unusual size" it said—and after the names I had learned to overhear, this one sounded almost friendly. It was only Goetz who persisted in holding his nose whenever he passed me. Once I almost forgot my resolution and approached him threateningly. But one of my coworkers, a man, incidentally, with the fanciest twirled mustache I have ever seen (you see, we had quite an assortment of oddities in our basement menagerie), warned me.

"Whoever starts a fight here at Fischer's is fired," he told me. "It doesn't matter who is right and who is wrong. That's the rule of the house."

At five minutes past six I took my position under

the Third Avenue Elevated, by the big clock of the Cooper Union. As I had left the building, quite a few of the basement brigade had departed with a cheery "So long, Jumbo"—and it had done my heart a lot of good. But now Goetz came down the street. When he walked by I stepped forward. He hadn't seen me before.

He didn't greet me. He just continued to walk.

"I want to talk to you, Herr Goetz," I said.

"What do you want, *sauhund?*"

"I want to ask you to stop insulting me."

"I'll talk to you the way I want. What are you going to do about it, you stinking Polack?"

And his hand went up to hold his nostrils.

Half a minute later he lay flat on his face. I had knocked his hand from his face and, as he tried to strike back, one of my favorite and never-failing wrestling combinations had suddenly and quite instinctively come back to my mind: a slap on the chest with the right hand and a crack with the right foot above the adversary's heel. There is just nothing a man can do in such a vise but fall on his back or on his face, whichever he prefers. Goetz chose the face.

The next morning the basement was buzzing with excitement. Goetz—a few nice black marks on his oversized face—was seen in conference with Hoffmann. Hoffmann left. He came back a little while later. Triumphantly he asked me to come upstairs to see the boss, Mr. Fischer. Goetz joined us gleefully. The boss didn't take long to pronounce judgment.

"You know the rules of the house," he said to me. "Whoever starts a fight leaves. Maybe this will teach you a lesson for your next job. Here you are through."

The others turned but I didn't move.

"Mr. Fischer," I said with all the desperate courage I could muster, "this man has been tormenting and humiliating me ever since I came here. I knew the rule and I didn't break it. I didn't hit him during working hours. I hit him six minutes past six—and outside, on Third Avenue."

Fischer turned towards Hoffmann and Goetz. They suddenly didn't look so good any more. "Is that so?" the old man snapped.

"We control our people from eight to six from Monday to Saturday," he said, pronouncing every word with the didactic concentration of a German professor. "What happens to them before eight or after six or on Sunday is none of my business. Get out of here—all three of you."

The men in the basement were overawed when they saw me whom they had thought doomed beyond redemption come back and take up my work again. Nobody ever mentioned the incident again. But I suddenly carried my head a little higher, and did my work once in a while with a smile. The next day I had my pay envelope.

I had six dollars in my pocket.

I had victoriously survived the most difficult week of my life.

I was happy.

There is an old saying in the old country: "If one is happy he feels like dancing."

And dancing I went.

It was Sunday morning. The street was deserted. Even the stoop was empty in the bright wintry sun. I entered the candy store at the corner, took out a dollar bill and put it on the counter.

"A pack of Sweet Caps—and a pack of cigarette paper." I had already learned that you could break a cigarette into two halves, and then roll the tobacco again in your own paper and make two out of it. Through an investment of one cent in a pack of cigarette paper the twenty Sweet Caps were easily transformed into forty Max Winkler specials—a little on the thin side and rather fast burning but sweet enough and oh, so cheap....

The lady at the counter looked at my dollar bill. She seemed worried.

"I got a job," I told her. "Remember the postcard you sold me? I sent it out and a letter came back and now I have a job."

She smiled. I told her that I was working in a big music house, and that it was a wonderful job, just the thing I had hoped for with all my heart, and that one day soon, maybe, I was going to be a music publisher myself. I told her that I had already met the big boss, old man Fischer himself—he, too, had begun somewhere in a basement—and now look at him!

She listened with great attention and seriousness.

"I think it s wonderful," she said at last, handing me my cigarettes and my paper and ninety-four cents in change.

"You can pay me the eighteen cents you owe me next Saturday. This is your first pay. Keep it. You'll need it."

It was a lovely Sunday. I walked out of the store and called Dave. We walked down Rivington Street and looked in the store windows. We looked at the pants in the windows and at the pants we were wearing. The store owners, leaning in their doors and calling out for customers, did the same. We sure looked like two customers, ready for the kill.

But we just walked by, smiling contemptuously as we heard sweet sales talk turn into sour abuse. We weren't interested in new pants. Tomorrow we were going to open our first bank account! After we had paid our rent and provided for a reasonable if not lavish down payment on Aunt Minnie's backlog of feeding bills, we saw ourselves in the possession of a cash capital of $2.08. We decided to treat ourselves to a glass of seltzer water with strawberry syrup. Here we smoked one of my specials and drank our drinks and talked of our bank account and of the promise we had made to our parents to bring the whole family together. Dave told me about the vicious dogs that attacked him regularly on his rounds and had made his pants such a sorry sight, and I told him about Mr. Hoffmann and Mr. Goetz.

"Dave," I said at last, "I think I am going down to Avenue B."

"Why?" said Dave.

"I want to see my girl."

"Your girl—"

"Sure. Hulda. Hulda from Radautz. Why don't you come along?"

But Dave wasn't in a romantic mood. Dave went to Delancey Street to see a movie in a Nickelodeon and I went to 46 Avenue B to see Hulda on the third floor. I did as much brushing, fixing and shining as my shoes and garments still could take and with a fresh shave on my cheeks and a song in my heart I walked down the Avenue. A grumpy woman I met in the hall of No. 46 told me that Hulda lived in apartment 9. The hall smelled heavily of stuffed cabbage. I began climbing up the stairs.

On the second floor I stopped. I had written Hulda before we had left home. That was nearly three months ago. Was she expecting me? How would she look after these years? I remembered her as a chubby, smiling redhead. She had been fifteen when I had seen her last.

A heavy smell of herring coming out of apartment 5 chased me up the stairs. I found No. 9. Suddenly I was filled with a choking fear. I couldn't get myself to ring the bell. I looked at my shabby clothes, my shoes that were beginning to show the rigors of the New York winter. Why had I come here?

I still didn't move. Suddenly the door of the apartment opened and in the semidarkness of the hall I saw a tall, fattish girl, a fuzzy mane of red hair, slippers without heels. Through the door behind her came the steaming smell of noodles. It was Hulda.

"Look who is here!" she screamed. "I thought you were dead."

She turned around. "It's Maaax!" She pronounced the name like a fox, howling it with a sustained hold that seemed to echo through the hallway.

I followed her into a room of medium size. It was filled with girls: girls sitting on the sofa, girls standing around in corners, girls chatting away, giggling, all holding glasses with steaming tea. Somewhere in a corner I saw a solitary man.

As soon as I entered the noise subsided. Complete silence filled the room. I just stood—and everybody turned and looked at me. For a short second I felt like laughing when I thought that I had come all the way, four thousand and more miles from Bucovina, had undergone cold and hunger and hardships of all kinds, had been arrested by the Austrian police and almost drowned on the S. S. *Gerty,* had starved and frozen—for this very moment, for this reunion with my Hulda! Then the tableau broke up. Everybody resumed their conversation; nobody paid the slightest attention to me.

I gathered that I had stepped into a party. I saw several of Hulda's sisters. Hulda herself had gone over and sat down next to the lonely man. He was the family's boarder. His name was Steiner. I began to hate him at once.

I was still standing at the door when Hulda's mama appeared in a cloud of steam.

"Hello, Maaax! Come out in the kitchen, I am busy cooking. How are things home?"

I could have kissed her. I followed her, sat down on a stool near the stove and began telling her. She didn't seem to listen. I soon stopped and just sat there, enjoying the heat of the coal fire, trying to figure out how I could get out of here. The only way out was through the living room. I heard again the chatting and giggling of the girls, Steiner's deep basso and Hulda screaming with delight at something he had said. The mother, too, had left the kitchen. I was alone, my face in both hands, gazing at the floor.

Then I heard a step. I looked up. A girl had come in from the party. I saw two friendly eyes, set in a round and smiling face.

She had a glass of tea and a plate with some cake.

"I thought you would like to have something to eat."

I drank the tea eagerly. But I couldn't eat. I felt crushed.

She sat down on an old broken chair and watched me empty the glass.

"So you are an old friend of Hulda's," the girl said.

I felt like denying it violently, like explaining that it was all a terrible mistake.

"Yes, sure, I am an old friend of hers," I said instead.

Maybe it sounded a little bitter because she smiled understandingly.

"Where do you live?" she said, changing the subject.

"Right nearby, on St. Mark's Place. Why do you ask?"

"Oh, for no particular reason. Just inquisitive."

"Thanks anyway. What is your name?"

"Clara. I live right here in the house, in the apartment downstairs. I came up to celebrate Bertha's birthday. And you are Max—what Max?"

We both smiled. I had forgotten the party next door and Hulda and Steiner and I didn't smell any noodles any more. I told her where I came from and about the S.S. *Gerty* and Dave, my twin.

"If you meet me on the street and I don't say hello, please don't be peeved at me. It wasn't me—it was Dave."

We had a lovely time. At last a girl stuck her head into the kitchen. It was Bertha, the birthday child.

"Clara, where are you?"

"I'll be right with you. Say, Bertha, let me have a needle and some black thread."

Bertha just shook her head but she came back presently with a little case. Clara took it, put it on the floor next to her and took out a few needles. She searched through a mess of loose pieces of thread and finally selected one.

"Have you got the buttons from your vest?" she asked me.

"Sure, I got them." I felt wonderful. "Here they are. They've been in my pocket almost since I left Radautz."

Clara began sewing and I watched her in silence. Inside we could hear Steiner making a birthday speech and then the voices rising to a toast and settling down again in never-ending waves of chatter. I just sat there, feeling Clara's hand close to my heart and wondering why I hadn't torn off a couple more buttons on that vest before I had come here.

After she had finished we both got up.

"Thank you," I said. "I can never tell you what you have done to me. I haven't seen much kindness lately." And then, with a little urgency: "I wish I could see you again."

"Maybe we'll meet again. Who knows? . . ."

"Thanks again for fixing my vest," I said in an effort to stall for time.

"I was glad to do it. You will look much better to the boss when you come to work tomorrow morning. Where do you work?"

"Do you know the big music store on Cooper Square?" I said proudly.

"Sure. I pass it every morning on my way to work," she replied. "I work with my sisters in a dress factory on Twelfth Street and Broadway."

"What time do you pass our store?"

"About 7:30."

"Would you mind if I say hello to you tomorrow morning? I start working at eight. I'm always hanging around at half past seven."

"That will be nice."

"Good-by. See you in the morning."

"Good-by."

I opened the door to the living room. Nobody seemed to notice me and I didn't care. I just walked towards the door and out in the hall.

On the street I took off my hat and let the brisk winter air stroke my temples. Then I began to whistle the "Washington Post," as if I had never carried 1850 pounds of it to a fifth floor on Cooper Square. I marched and swung my hat and whistled.

I had a job.

I had a girl.

I had a bank account.

I had nothing in the world to worry about.

5.

Winter was over. Spring had come.

The people on the stoop at St. Mark's Place began to take in the early sun and the late sun—and presently, as the first waves of New York heat began to attack our tenement, their meetings would last deep into the night. Clara and I met every morning before work and walked together a few blocks; and soon we would also meet at night, walking through the milling crowds as happy and alone as if this noisy, boiling city had been an island somewhere in the blue South Seas.

On Sunday we would take the Franklin Avenue trolley to Coney Island. You would first take a streetcar across the bridge and then the trolley down to the beach. The trolley cars were open—seats running the length of the car and boards to put your feet on. After you had squeezed your girl onto a seat you hung dangling from the board—all the one and a half hours down to the beach. But what were the terrors of a Brooklyn streetcar to me who had learned to hold on the much harder way when I was racing down the mountains on our miniature railroad back home....

Back home? I could sense almost from day to day, from hour to hour how home wasn't back there in Europe any more, how home began to be here. Home was the room I still shared with brother Dave on the fifth floor, home was the basement at Cooper Square where now I knew every corner and every niche and every protruding piece of steel. Home were the fellows I shared my days with—Goetz and Schwebel and old man Roemhild with his magic tube and even Mr. Hoffmann who had given me a raise without my having dared to ask for one. Home was the bench in Seventh Street Park where Clara and I sat once in a while talking about the past, the present and the future. We were both of the same age—both nineteen years young.

"I think it's wonderful!" I had said when we had first found out.

"Why?"

"Because we can grow old together."

That was all. Nothing else was said. But it was never forgotten.

Only once the full impact of what home had once meant came back with sudden agonizing pain. We had gone for a picnic with a few of the fellows from the office, their wives and sweethearts. A ferryboat took us across, again past the Statue of Liberty that now looked so different in the bright colors of the summer day, to Staten Island. There we stepped ashore and walked a little while. Suddenly my foot touched grass. Soft, cool grass. I walked as if in a trance. Everybody seemed to watch me. I blushed.

I suddenly realized that I hadn't touched grass since I had left my mother's house. . . .

But soon the grass was forgotten and the foot

walked firmly on stone and heat and cement. Home
was here. Not that there were welcome signs and
garlands all over the place. The New York of 1907
was a very different place from the friendly city of
today; and as for the many committees that today
welcome the newcomer—well, let me tell you of one
of the many welcoming committees for greenhorns
in the year of our Lord 1907. That one greeted Dave
and me on a rainy Sunday afternoon as we were
strolling up the Bowery. We passed one of the many
shooting galleries. We stopped, looked, and entered.
TEST YOUR STRENGTH, a big sign invited—and what
better game could there be for two Rumanian lumberjacks? It was a contraption with two handles. As
you pressed them together a hand on a dial indicated
your progress: 10—25—50—100. I inserted a penny
and began to press. The hand moved. It moved rapidly from 100 to 200. It moved slowly from 200 to 400.

"I bet you a nickel you can't get maximum," Dave
said.

I couldn't reply. Through grinding teeth I moaned
an acceptance of his challenge and pushed with all
my strength. A bell rang. The hand had touched 500.
I let go and proudly turned towards Dave.

"You owe me a nickel," I said.

"You owe me two dollars and fifty cents," a voice
said—and it wasn't Dave speaking. It was an attendant, a very tall and very powerful attendant, who
spoke. And suddenly there were three more attendants. I hadn't seen any of them before. Now they
were just standing there, silently staring at us.

"You heard the bell, mister," the first attendant said, scarcely moving his lips. His voice made an ugly grinding sound. "You hit 500. That's half a cent a point. Come on. Pay up."

It wasn't much of a fight. Greenhorns in those days didn't call a cop and didn't yell for help. Greenhorns looked at three silent attendants and took out their last week's pay and paid up and left. Greenhorns went silently home through the rain and if they had any sense they weren't even mad. They put down the two dollars and fifty cents as an initiation fee to the life in the Big City.

Two dollars and fifty cents, though, was a tough price to pay for whatever knowledge and wisdom it bought. My salary now was $8.50. Of this I paid a nickel to Carl Fischer's *Krankenunterstuetzungsverein* (don't start counting: the word has twenty-eight letters and it means something like "mutual sickness insurance"). But then, I didn't pay anything to the U.S. Government which had not yet eaten from the evil apple Income Tax! So I took home every week the amount of $8.45. Here is what I did with it:

Room and breakfast $1.50

    (Breakfast consisted of a cup of coffee and two rolls and was usually brought in by a little kid so dirty that I couldn't touch the food. This was, as I found out later, an ingenious device of the landlady to get her two rolls back.)

Supper at Aunt Minnie's   2.50

Lunch	.18

(Sounds amazing but wasn't. Two cents would buy half a round loaf of bread, two days old and thus reduced in price. One cent would get three slightly rotten apples from a pushcart. But cutting out the rotten parts I could get two or at least one and a half eatable ones. That makes three cents a day for lunch.)

Cigarettes and cigarette paper	.12
Assorted Luxuries	.25
	$4.55

This left $3.90 which, every Monday morning, went to the Dry Dock Savings Bank.

It was a happy life. Dave had left his coffee peddler and was now wearing the cap of a streetcar conductor. He was working for the Metropolitan Railway Company, collecting nickels on one of the many horse-drawn cars that were rattling through the streets of New York. The cars were about twenty feet long. They had four wheels on two axles, both centered in the middle of the car. Both ends, utterly unsupported, hung out in the air.

During rush hours these cars, built for some twenty-five passengers, carried a hundred and more. Fifty were inside, packed like sardines, only less comfortable: they didn't float in oil and the rubbing was something bone-breaking. The rest of the passengers were hanging on outside. Every time the horses began to move with a sudden jerk and/or every time the car slowed down as the brakes were applied with another jerk, a tremor went through the poor

car, starting in front, rolling on like an earthquake
and ending up in a furious tremolo in the rear. No
dog shaking off a cloud of fleas could ever have done
so with more devastating success than did these cars,
shaking off their passengers. Soon the part that had
shaken off most of them and thus had become light
began to rise while the opposite half almost touched
the ground. If a car then hit a curve the passengers
on both ends were simply shot off into space.

Dave had nothing to do with the horses. He was
just a conductor, the so-called "collector of fares."
Every time he collected a nickel he was supposed to
pull a string that jerked a lever that jerked a meter
that rang a bell. The bell announced to the world
that Dave had collected a nickel for the Metropolitan
Railway Company. But the bell rang only seldom.
The string was inside the car. The collector of fares,
unable to squeeze through the sardines, was balancing outside on the running boards, hanging on for
dear life. I don't know how they could ever afford it,
but the Metropolitan Railway Company paid Dave
each Saturday $11.45. On Monday we went together
to the Dry Dock Savings Bank.

From Jack we heard little. He was still in Port
Jervis, working on the Erie Railroad. He, too, had a
bank account. Once in a while we felt like millionaires.

Not always, though, were economics as simple and
easy as that. It was all right to go to the bank every
Monday and to remember what we had promised
our father and mother, and to write to them that

slowly but surely we would be able to send for them as we had said we would. But then the evening came when I was to take Clara to the movies for the first time. I had done some real brushing up for the event. I had borrowed Dave's new shoes—the collector of fares had just bought a beautiful new pair. As he had left the shoe store the right heel had come off—right there, in front of the store and in view of the salesman who had come to the door to see him off. Dave went right back, limping on one heel and protesting furiously with the little English he knew and three of the salesmen—the "three attendants" seemed to be everywhere in this strange new world—had thrown him out while uttering words that didn't restore his heel but certainly increased the English vocabulary of the collector of fares.

However, the heel had been fixed, the shoes were on my feet, and I had two dimes, the balance of this week's account "Assorted Luxuries," safely tucked away in my pocket.

"I told everybody that you were taking me to the movies," Clara said as we met in front of her house on Avenue B and I proudly took her arm. "Everybody," that much I knew already, was Papa and Mama and six sisters—and it made me feel big and strong and happy to know that this was an official outing and that six sisters, as in a fairy tale, were envying Cinderella her cavalier.

And so we arrived at the Fourteenth Street Theater and I stepped forward to the ticket window and pushed my two dimes through the little opening.

"This one is a Canadian dime," the girl behind the window said and pushed it right back.

And there was the big, strong prince staring in crushing desperation at a Canadian dime and Cinderella breaking out in a friendly, understanding smile and taking a dime out of her little purse and taking her cavalier to the movies. It worked out all right, and later on our bench in Seventh Street Park, it was all forgotten. But it had been a harsh lesson in economics and one I would never forget in all my life. Soon, an even graver financial matter reared its ugly head.

When Clara told me one day shortly afterwards that it would be nice if I could come up to the house and meet her people I looked down at the suit I had brought with me from Radautz. The two buttons Clara had sewed on, that fateful Sunday, had been followed by many more that had gone and had never been replaced. The suit had battled the sharp edges of Bin No. 369 in the Fischer basement—and had lost the battle ignominiously. It had absorbed the dust of hundreds of packages. It had gone through winter and spring. It was still good enough for a day with Goetz and Schwebel, but no matter how you looked at it, it wasn't good enough any more to go a-visiting.

I went into a huddle with Dave and Aunt Minnie. Conferences of a complicated financial nature went on for several days. It was Sunday again when, $11.60 firmly tucked away in an inner pocket (it, too, had to be mended for the seventh time by patient Minnie before I went on my mission) and determined to put an absolute minimum of ten dollars on my purchase, I went down to Canal Street to buy a suit.

Canal Street was the busiest thoroughfare I had ever seen in my life. It was filled with a maze of horse-drawn vehicles. Once in a while a gaily painted open motorcar, its horn bleating incessantly and scaring horses and men alike, wormed its way through the traffic. Pushcarts overflowing from Orchard and Essex Street displayed an inexhaustible variety of merchandise, veritable department stores on two wheels. One of them offered oranges, mountains of them, and as I passed it I stopped. Ever since my father had once brought home a few oranges, a rare delicacy in our mountains, the fruit had had a strange fascination for me. The peddler at once spotted me and came over.

"Oranges," he yelled, "beautiful oranges. Three cents a piece. Because it's you, young fellow, I let you have three for a dime."

I took out a dime and bought three oranges. Only after the peddler had disappeared in the crowd did I realize how he had duped me. The greenhorn-welcoming committee was again at work! But I didn't mind. I laughed. A penny as another initiation fee wasn't too much, after all, not even for me.

As I walked slowly up the street, munching one of my three-and-one-third-cent oranges, I passed hundreds of bright windows filled with suits, pants, shirts, hats and ties. Canal Street was known in those days as Suit Hunting Avenue. It was a man's street, quite exclusive. There wasn't a single store where a woman could have bought anything but a tie for a husband.

Many of the windows were filled with magnificent dummies, all reflecting the high life of society. They were dressed beautifully in suits of all shades. Some of them seemed to promenade in serene Fifth Avenue elegance. Others were sitting leisurely, smoking cigarettes in ivory holders, petting poodles, reading splendidly bound books. Still others sported magnificent derbies or were engaged in serious conversation, leaning nonchalantly on elegant canes.

Outside, in front of the stores, were the hawkers.

"Hey, mister," they barked, and their cries overcut each other and filled the street with a constant staccato of human voices. "Hey, mister, it's a suit you want. And if it's a suit you want this is the place to get it."

If you as much as hesitated the hawker would run over and grab your arm and place his arm around your neck and in friendly tones, but backed up by an overpowering embrace, would keep on talking while he marched you away.

And so, attracted at last beyond the call of prudence by a monocled dummy with a gray derby ($2.75) and a begloved right hand, I hesitated just one second too long. A hawker jumped. I was a goner.

He took hold of my left arm and we began to walk. As we entered the store I found that there was none. There was just a window with all the beautiful things to look at and a door that led down to the basement. As we climbed down the stairs the hawker cried out:

"Abe! Customer!"

We had reached the cellar. The hawker didn't let go of my arm till a cigar-chewing man in shirt sleeves had gotten hold of the right one. Then he returned to the upper world. Abe escorted me deeper to the back of the store room, which was filled with all kinds of clothing.

"All right, pal," he said, and his voice that seemed to come out of a rusty barrel filled with gravel made me shrink back, "all right, pal, we have just the thing for you."

He pulled a suit from a pile.

"Take off your pants," he thundered. I took off my pants.

Abe watched me silently, chewing wildly at his cigar. He seemed to lose patience with me.

"Come on now!" he roared. "Give me your pants. Try these."

I put on the pants he had handed me. They were at least five inches too short.

"Mister," I said timidly, "these pants, don't you think they are a little bit short?"

Abe's face contorted in a vicious grin. "Short—well, you sure must be a greenhorn. Don't you know that's the way they wear 'em now in America?"

I looked again down my legs and tried to make a step forward. The trousers were as tight as cement.

"I don't want them," I said. "I don't think I want any new suit today. Let me have my pants."

Abe seemed unimpressed.

"O.K., O.K., pal," he said. "Take it easy now, don't get excited. Hey, Moe! Where are his pants?"

Moe—I hadn't seen or heard Moe before—emerged out of the dark.

"What pants?" he said. "Whose pants?" He was tiny and thin, a fraction only of bulging Abe. But he had a flat nose and cauliflower ears and I didn't like Moe a bit.

"This fellow here," Abe said. "He says he can't find his pants."

"Look, mister," Moe said. Then he broke up in the middle of whatever sentence he had started to hurl at me. "Ah, what the hell!" he said, turned and vanished in the dark.

Abe spat out what was left of his cigar, took out a new one and lit it slowly.

"Don't worry, pal," he said at last. "Your pants must be around here some place, or maybe Philip sold them or maybe he put them some place. He just went out to make a delivery. Just wait here till Phil comes back—or maybe I'll find you in the meantime a suit with long pants. Look here: I got a good suit for you right here. Try on the jacket.

I put on the jacket. The sleeves barely covered my elbows.

I extended my bare forearms towards Abe in a silent gesture of despair and protest.

"What's the matter now?" Abe said. "Aren't short sleeves nicer than short pants? What else do you want?"

"I want my pants back."

"Here we go again. What do you worry? We got lots of pants. Hey, Moe, come here, fix his coat."

Moe came back. He scarcely glanced at the coat. "It can take an inch or two more," he said. "Take it off."

He ripped the coat off my body, took it and departed.

Abe, too, strolled away in an evil cloud of cigar smoke. I was alone.

Cautiously I began moving around. I had to find my pants. I had to get out of here. I looked at the tables and the shelves, I looked at the floor and up at the hangers. Pants, pants, pants—but I couldn't find mine. I was a thirsty sailor, marooned in the middle of the ocean, dying from thirst with oceans of water surrounding him.

Suddenly I heard Moe yell somewhere in the dark, "Where is he, where is the fellow you were selling the suit to?"

"I don't know," gravel voice answered. "He must be around here somewhere. He couldn't have run out without his pants."

"Who says he couldn't? He probably ran out with half a dozen pants. If I catch him I'll murder him. Get him, you dope, before he takes the whole place."

By now I was lost somewhere between the tailor shop way back in the basement and a dozen tables loaded with stacks of boxes up to the ceiling. I tried to find my way back to the spot from where I had started. But Moe's voice had trailed off and there was nothing to guide me. The place was filled with a sinister silence. I stood there, without pants, trying to figure out what to do next. My situation, I realized, was dangerously balancing between the ridiculous and the catastrophic.

After a little while I heard steps. Moe and Abe had returned and I heard little Moe pouring out a stream of invectives against mighty Abe who had "let the dirty robber get away with half the store."

Suddenly he turned a corner and saw me.

He was still holding my new coat with the lengthened sleeves over his arm.

"What are you doing here in the dark?" he growled. "Here is your new suit. Let me have the money and get the hell out of here."

"Let me have my pants."

Abe extended a lazy hand and pushed one of the cardboard boxes off a table. There were my pants.

I took them. I slipped on the new suit. It was a sun-bleached pale blue. The two inches at the end of the sleeves weren't quite so bleached and much more blue. I handed Moe the money, rushed up the stairs and with a deep breath stepped out into the bustle of the street. A man was offering oranges. But I just laughed at him, I wasn't buying any more. No, sir, not me. Not today and not tomorrow and not ever again.

The next morning at our regular 7:30 meeting I faced Clara in my new suit. She paled only slightly and then she smiled. We walked along our accustomed route. As we passed a big mirror in a furniture

store I suddenly saw myself for the first time in my
new American suit.

I looked at Clara with a reassured feeling of happiness. A girl that could see such a sight and still smile
had passed the supreme test of love and affection.
I took her arm and in the midst of the thunderous
traffic of Third Avenue bent down and kissed her.
Nothing that fate might ever have in store could ever
tear us apart.

And it was good to know it. Because the next
thing that fate had in store for me was my visit to
Clara's home, that same night. As I walked up the
stairs which I had ascended only a little while ago
when I had come to this same house eager to embrace my Hulda, I thought back to that humiliating
experience. What was going to happen tonight? What
was I doing here—an eight-fifty-a-week office boy in
Carl Fischer's basement? The smells of cabbage and
herring still lingered on the worn-out stairs. Suddenly I was filled with a terrorizing fear that now,
this very moment, Hulda would come down from
her fourth-floor apartment and that a cry of "Maaax"
would throw me completely off what little balance I
still had. But no Hulda appeared. On the third floor
I rang the bell. The door was opened at once. There
was Clara, her friendly smile on her friendly face;
she bade me come in.

I had known that I was to meet the mother and
had mentally steeled myself for just such an emergency. But I wasn't prepared for what faced me:

not one, but seven females, sitting on chairs and on a sofa—and every one of them looking at me. These must be Clara's six sisters in addition to the mother; and I knew at once that they weren't there by accident. There must have been some advance publicity, no doubt, and now every one of my words and moves would be judged by fourteen eyes and fourteen ears. I felt as comfortable as a man in a police line-up.

Clara mumbled an introduction. Seven heads nodded an acknowledgment. Nobody said a word.

At last one of them, the mother apparently, looked up from her knitting and said:

"Please sit down."

I looked around. There wasn't an empty chair in the room. I scraped the floor uneasily, feeling my lips break out in a hysterical smile of embarrassment and did the only thing I could do: I remained standing where I was.

"Reggie," the mother said, "let the gentleman have a chair."

Reggie got up. Mama, no doubt, was in full command of this house. Reggie gave me a look of violent resentment and it was clear that she had obeyed only under extreme mental strain. I had already made an enemy.

But this was no time for diplomatic finesse. I sat down, speechless, waiting for somebody to say something to someone. But nobody spoke. The mother's needles clicked noisily through the silence. The six sisters kept their eyes focused on me. The younger ones stared quite openly. The older ones looked and smiled like amateur actresses. The mother, whenever she looked up, gave me a piercing work-over. It was hell.

Isn't there a man in the house, I began to think. Seven girls must have at least one father. But if they had one he wasn't there. I was raised in a home where Father was master and final arbiter in everything and where the male population was five against a gentle mother and a little sister. Here the ratio was eight against one father who wasn't here, and right now it was eight to one against one befuddled "gentleman."

At last the mother ordered one of the younger girls —her name was Norah—to get up and get a glass of raspberry syrup and some cake "for the gentleman." Norah got up at once and disappeared into the kitchen. To the clicking of the needles were added Norah's steps in the kitchen, the bubbling of the raspberry syrup from the bottle to the glass, the opening and closing of drawers—but otherwise, still frozen and terrifying silence.

Norah returned after what appeared to me eternity. She carried two glasses of syrup, one for mother and one for myself and the ice, at last, seemed to break. Conversations got under way. Several girls from the neighborhood dropped in. The smaller fry was sent to bed. Mama put her knitting away and sat down next to Clara and me. She began asking me about myself and my people at home and how I had managed life in America so far and what I intended to do. She was a woman of medium height and very good-looking. As she spoke to me I felt her penetrating alertness, the experience of a woman who had looked at many things. At the same time she kept it all on a very casual plane, making it appear as if it really wasn't so important.

As the years passed on I saw a lot of Mama Yetta. I saw her in amazement and dazed admiration accomplish the nearly impossible with the greatest of ease: I saw her unload seven girls without a nickel's endowment with bewildering speed. During one single year, between the months of July and November, she disposed triumphantly of the last batch of three. As time went on all the girls grew bigger and all the husbands smaller and quieter. Whenever there was a special gathering in the family—and in a family of such magnificent proportions there were an unending number of gatherings throughout the year—Mama Yetta always made her entrance at the head of her seven married daughters. The husbands were left to gather meekly in a corner, obviously unworthy to participate in so magnificent a procession. At one such affair Mama established what might be an all time record: four of her girls were successively in the sixth, seventh, eighth and ninth month—a miraculous timing as this monthly succession even coincided with the ages of the prospective mothers. It was then, I believe, that one of the seven husbands, timidly raising his voice among six of his unfortunate brethren, exclaimed in a sudden outcry: "There goes Snow White and her seven dwarfs!" The name stuck to her forever, but there has never been a more flagrant misnomer: Mama to her last day was as dark as ebony, and the seven girls were of giant proportions. . . .

So the evening floated along gently. Only a few of the sisters had remained. I began almost to feel at home. Clara was sitting next to me. She, too, seemed to be happy and pleased. It must have been long after ten o'clock when the doorbell gave two short rings. "Here is Papa," one of the girls said and when the door opened I saw a small bearded man in the doorway. He seemed tired beyond description. One of the girls took his coat. He took a few uneasy steps and sank into a chair.

"Father," Clara said, "this is Max Winkler. He comes from the same part of Europe we come from."

Papa just nodded with a friendly smile. Then he kept his eyes closed for a few moments as if trying to gather what little strength was left in him. Mama called from the kitchen. He got up and I saw him stooped over a plate of soup, eating eagerly. I felt that it was time for me to leave. Clara walked me down the stairs. A little later as we were sitting for a while on one of our benches in the park she spoke about her father. She spoke tenderly and with a touching affection.

As I look back today I never remember Papa Max as a well man. But I remember him as a proud and strangely happy man. At the time I met him he was just reaching the age of fifty-five. But he looked twenty years older. His body was continuously racked by asthmatic coughs. His working day—he operated a little open-air stationery store—started at five in the morning and ended at ten at night. Through him I learned that you can preserve a pure heart and a fine mind and can enjoy the tender and beautiful things of life while you work in unending toil.

I loved to sit with him during long evenings in his little open-air store. Clara would wait on an occasional customer and I would talk to Papa Max. He knew not much about business or politics, but he knew all about human relations, about kindness, about love. The way he managed to survive the long hours in his store, the weary, slow and dragging walks in all seasons of the year, shall always remain with me an inspiring example of a proud and courageous heart. He would never admit to his family that he was tired and ill. The long walks, he said, were good for his health and an open-air store kept him fresh and alive. And he would wait on a customer, sell him a few cigarettes, or a piece of candy for a penny or two, and afterwards turn towards me and smile with his eyes. You couldn't see his lips, they were covered with the beard of a patriarch; but you would see the smile in his eyes and a gentle pride and a strange touching happiness. When the weather was bad and the customers few he would talk to me—about his home and his wife and his daughters, about what a home meant to a man and how you could find happiness in your own heart and contentment in your mind.

At last he had to give in—no walks to the "business" any more, no customers, no talks of wisdom. For months he had been in his bed, too weak to get up and now almost too weak to move. And then the day came when Papa looked up to the ceiling of his room and began to describe to us in hardly audible words the pictures of the paradise and the people he saw on that ceiling. For three days Papa Max was in heaven—and with him were all his children. He spoke of grandchildren he would never hold on his lap: he saw them all, building them beautiful homes, sharing unending riches with them. His words sounded like prayers of thanksgiving; the poor old man who all his life had toiled and worked and lived in heartbreaking poverty was giving thanks for a full life, and the good Lord made him see all his children, happily married, surrounded by their own children—smiling, happy and rich—and he and Mama Yetta among them, in every scene on that ceiling above. Happiness was in his heart and a great smile in his eyes as he closed them forever.

6.

The months passed on. My daily walks to Carl Fischer's music house at Cooper Square, the descent to the basement in the morning and the ascent, tired but never discouraged, after ten solid hours of back-breaking work, had become a beloved routine. I had dreamed about a job in music, I had fought desperately to get it when I saw my chance—and *now* I had it: I was sweeping floors, I was wiping up dust, I lighted and extinguished gas lights and, more than anything else, I carried heavy packages from the ground to a table and from a table to a shelf and then back from the shelf to the table and from the table to the ground. But I didn't despair. Ever since I had heard that old man Fischer, the mighty boss himself, had started out in a little basement, back in 1872, I was determined to stick it through. Of one thing I was sure, at least: I would always be able to say truthfully that I had learned the music business from the bottom up! And soon my first break came. Music at last made its triumphant entrance into my life.

It was due to the prolonged illness of a man by the name of Bebel, one of the laziest members of the basement brigade, that Mr. Hoffmann, who must have been watching me for some time, suddenly put me in charge of the collating department. It was still a job based on packages, but now for the first time I wasn't only to carry them—I could open them, see what was inside, look at clean white sheets of paper, touch and handle what I had come here to touch and to handle: music.

The job—I even had two assistants to help me!—was to transform these large and bulky packages of band and orchestra music into small units. One package, for example, would contain five hundred copies of Tenor Trombones to Sousa's "Semper Fidelis." Another, five hundred Piccolos. But the copy of the march that was to be sold to the ultimate consumer was to contain only one copy of these instruments. And here is where the collating department came in.

Now I began to understand the meaning of the very long tables I had seen near Hoffmann's desk at my first appearance down there. They were collating tables. Soon I learned that a Standard Military Band copy contained twenty-eight different instrument parts, a Full Band copy forty-eight but a Symphonic Band not less than seventy-six and sometimes as many as eighty-five different parts. So you would bring in twenty-eight or forty-eight or eighty-five different packages. You would stack them in proper rotation on the collating table—Piccolo, Flute, four different Clarinets, all kinds of Cornets and Trumpets, the Bugles and the French Horns, Altos and Mellophones, Baritones, Trombones in several clefs, Tubas and then the Drums and Cymbals, the Tambourines and Xylophones, the Chimes and Bells, and sometimes a part for sandpaper or pistol.

The parts were stacked on the table and then you began to walk. You started at the right corner and walked down the length of the table and you turned and kept on walking and turning till you came back to where you had started. During the trip you picked up sheet after sheet, sometimes one, sometimes two or more for the same instrument, and when you had completed your circle you had completed a unit, a "band copy," and you handed it to another man who put a cover around it and then put it on a stack, and after he had assembled a hundred or two hundred of these units the man would make a heavy package out of them and would take it from the ground to a table and from the table to a shelf and later on, after an inch or two of nice black dust had gathered on it, he would take it again from the shelf to a table and from the ʈable—oh, what the hell.

And so I was walking around the collating table from morning till night, five hundred rounds a day. You would pick up 30,000 sheets in the course of the day and to do so you had to wet your fingers 30,000 times. You would first wet them on the tip of your tongue and as the tip dried up your fingers would go deeper and deeper until at the end of the day your tongue was numb and your throat parched and your chest filled with dust and printers' ink.

But there were errands. The little dumb-waiters connecting the basement with the store broke down ever so often and angry voices hollering through the magic tubes made the damned from the depths rush to the upper regions. You delivered your load to one of the clerks behind the counters and then, when you had a little luck, you could hear Mr. Hartmann, a tall man with a floating tie and an impressive, very artistic mane of silvery hair, demonstrate a violin to a customer. There was a big pillar right next to the violin counter where I would hide for a few minutes and listen in fascination to Mr. Hartmann's fiddle. He put all the demonic power and the technical brilliance of a Paganini on a four-dollar violin, ending his grandiose demonstration with a most elegant sweep of the bow. It all was magnificent and yet seemed so easy when you listened to him. One of his favorite pieces was Bach's Air on the G String and whenever an eager customer asked how he managed to do it he would say with his heavy Swiss accent: "There is nothing to it. Just put your finger on the string and schlide it down." Hartmann—as did everything and everybody up there—filled me who had never been inside a concert hall with envy and admiration. I would stand there and listen till a hollow voice from the basement drew me back to the depths.

On other occasions I would watch a frail young man in the instrument department demonstrate trumpets. He made them sing and quaver in brilliant cadenzas and sombre march tunes and people would gather around him all day and make him do it all over again after he had finished because it sounded so nice. His name was Edwin Franko Goldman. He became my friend later, much later, when we met on a different plane of life and when many more people gathered around him because the music he made—on the Mall—sounded so nice. . . . Sometimes I would spot Fritz Kreisler whose name and face I had seen on posters on my way to work, a tall imposing figure of a young man, come in the place and walk up to old man Fischer's private office. His tunes and arrangements were just beginning to become popular and Fischer's were Kreisler's American publishers. And there was Leopold Auer, the great teacher of great fiddlers, and his pupils, young Elman, young Heifetz, young Toscha Seidel—all Fischer composers, all steady visitors, all an inspiring sight to the anonymous boy from the basement who watched them and decided to work harder and harder so that maybe, one day, he too would work up there and say hello to John Philip Sousa and listen to Hartmann's fiddle without hiding in fear behind a pillar.

Even through the dumb-waiters and tubes came the sound of the trumpet and the sweeping melodies of the fiddle, dripping down to the basement as we made our dreary rounds around the collating tables like buffaloes trotting around a water well. There also came the sound from some of the Edison Phonographs that had been installed upstairs, playing the latest novelties for the customers: the early tunes of Irving Berlin, "Everybody's Doing It" and "Alexander's Ragtime Band," sweet Viennese serenades, "Love Me and the World is Mine," and an unending wave of so-called "Hesitation Waltzes," the fad of the day. We hummed the music as we walked around the table.

Slowly I began to get a feeling for the complicated and fascinating machinery that makes a music publishing house tick. I saw the editors and arrangers at work, the sales managers and traveling salesmen getting their instructions, the pluggers and the men in charge of production. I even saw old man Fischer, the boss, when he came to the basement from time to time, turning off gas lights that weren't absolutely necessary to prevent us from breaking our necks in the dark or asking us to open bales of waste paper again. If he found a single sheet of paper in one of these bales that he thought could still be flattened out and used again, murder was in his eyes.

The editors' offices were piled with manuscripts. It seemed incredible to my peeking eyes to see how many people wrote music—songs and piano pieces, hymns and marches, studies for the piccolo—everything under the sun. Every day we saw the mailman bring in stacks of these manuscripts, and every day we saw stacks go out again, back to the ministers in Sioux City and the housewives in New Hope who had written them with their very heart's blood and who now got them back with form letter No. 3. One of these unnamed thousands who fancied themselves neglected geniuses worked right here among us, a member of the basement brigade. Every day he would show us a new opus he had written the night before, would hum the tune for us, would talk about the fame and the wealth that were sure to be his if he could only make Mr. Saenger, the chief editor upstairs, open that door marked *Private* and look at his works. At last Hoffmann—more concerned to be sure with the waning efficiency of one of his buffaloes than with a young composer's bid for fame —promised to take one of his manuscripts "upstairs." Parker (this was the young man's name—I can still see him, thin, tall, with ecstatic eyes) was completely overwhelmed. His usefulness as a buffalo went down to zero. The climax came when an infuriated salesman from the orchestra department rushed down into the cellar—something unheard of, upstairs salesmen just wouldn't mingle with the devils of the underworld—to throw an orchestra copy at Hoffmann. Parker, his mind already wandering in the clouds of immortality, had made up a unit that consisted of Flute parts to the "Blue Danube," Clarinet parts to Ivanovici's "Waves of the Danube," and Trumpet parts taken from Juvenito Rosa's "Danube Waves."

For days there was no reply. Parker had chosen, after hours of tormenting deliberation, to submit what he considered his masterpiece: a song whose words and music he had written and which he called the "Subway Waltz." He had recited and hummed it to us, we all thought it beautiful and great and now we all suffered with Parker the tormenting pains of waiting. Every time somebody would come down the stairs the buffaloes stopped rotating, their eyes fixed to the stairs, only to see an insignificant office boy emerge with a stack of insignificant music. At

last, one day after lunch, Mr. Hoffmann appeared
with a large envelope. He handed it to Parker. It
contained the manuscript of the "Subway Waltz."

Parker took it. He opened it sheepishly, searching
for a message. There was none.

Then Hoffmann spoke. "Mr. Saenger asked me to
give you back your 'Subway Waltz.' They think the
words are beautiful but the air is rotten."

The Bard of the Subways never got the joke. He
just took his manuscript, put it on a chair in a
corner and went back to stack No. 17, E flat Altos,
where he had left off. The buffalo was back in his
yoke.

This was my first experience with the heartbreaking
lot of a composer. As time passed on I would meet
hundreds of Parkers and look with amazement at
thousands of Subway Waltzes, but none of them ever
would appear to me quite as pathetic as this young
man with the ecstatic eyes with his crushed dreams
of beauty and happiness.

Disaster and disappointment, however, were not
the only events the collating department would take
active part in. We were just as alert to the electrifying consequences of success. Whenever a best seller
exploded we would note its appearance by the fact
that instead of changing our stacks of piccolo and
mellophone parts every two or three hours we would
continue making units of one and the same piece for
days and weeks on end. Soon we collated the infernal
tune in every possible combination—in standard band

and symphonic band, in orchestrations with and without piano, in trios and quartets. I watched these hits with eagerness. There was a simple business logic! What had to be collated most was selling best. I walked around the table, thinking and wondering about the music business.

One of these electrifying events was the appearance of "Hearts and Flowers" by Theodore Moses Tobani in the Fischer catalogue. Here I could study in a perfect, almost scientific demonstration the elements of a success. Tobani was a composer on the permanent staff of Fischer's. I had rubbed my aching shoulders on hundreds of his arrangements. There wasn't a waltz by Strauss, a polka by Waldteufel, a tune by Ivanovici, an overture by Suppé, that wasn't known throughout America in a Tobani arrangement. When Tobani wrote "Hearts and Flowers"—the word "wrote" has to be taken with a grain of salt as will presently be seen—nobody thought much of it. It was just another Tobani tune. But within a few months there wasn't a sentimental vaudeville act in the country that didn't use it, not a barbershop quartet that didn't sing it, not a burlesque act that didn't parody it. It was a tremendous hit for many years to come and still, today, it's one of the sentimental tunes everybody seems to know. An avalanche of "Hearts and Flowers" overwhelmed the basement. Bins and bins were filled with every conceivable combination of the tune. Through the dumb-waiters came "Hearts and Flowers" from morning to night. Parker seemed near collapse. Here was a

fellow worker right here at Fischer's who had everything a composer could dream of, fame and money
galore; while he, Parker, was condemned forever to
trot around a collating table.

Soon, however, Parker's attitude changed. There
was an ugly grin of devilish delight on his face and
it changed into a smirk of triumph every time he had
to collate still another arrangement of "Hearts and
Flowers." Parker had found out what soon had become common knowledge throughout the building:
Theodore Moses Tobani did not share a single penny
in the overwhelming financial success of "Hearts and
Flowers." Theodore Moses Tobani was an arranger
on Fischer's payroll and whatever he arranged or
composed was their property, complete and forever
and with no strings attached. Parker got paid for
walking around a table and Theodore Moses got paid
for composing tunes. He had composed. He had been
paid. And that was all there ever was to it.

As did everybody else I considered all this a
flagrant case of spiritual exploitation. I looked at it
however with a somewhat changed attitude when, a
few years later, I glanced absent-mindedly at a copy
of an old piece by Alphons Czibulka that Fischer's
had imported from Europe. It was called "Love and
Roses" and subtitled "A Flower Song." As I looked
at the melody my mind returned from its absence
with a vengeance. The piece, there couldn't be any
doubt, was "Hearts and Flowers," note by note and
bar by bar!

All these experiences and their moral and financial

implications made a deep impression on me. The potentialities of the music trade seemed tremendous. In my dreams I heard Edwin Franko Goldman, Parker's ecstatic eyes in his friendly face, playing "Hearts and Flowers" on a silvery trumpet; and during the day, when I heard the music coming down the dumb-waiters, I smiled. I wasn't in a hurry to get up there. I had time. I knew that I wouldn't miss.

The first Monday of January, 1908, had begun pleasant and uneventful. The weekly walk to the Dry Dock Savings Bank to make the accustomed deposit had started it off. The man had added a few dollars of interest—the first money I had ever earned without working for it and it made me feel good to look at the bankbook. My balance was approaching the two-hundred mark! Then, a little later, I had met Clara as I had every day and we had walked through the icy wind of the winter morning the few blocks to work. The usual share of toil and abuse, the consoling droplets of music coming through the dumb-waiters—nothing to single out this particular day as anything but just another day in a busy, unworried, almost happy life.

But as I went home and was walking up the stairs to Aunt Minnie's for supper I heard excited voices. Inside there was Minnie, all flushed and agitated, and Dave the collector of fares walking around the kitchen, talking and gesticulating wildly. Aunt Minnie's three daughters had retired to a corner of the living room, three timid chickens waiting for a

storm to pass. The dinner table wasn't set and the
kitchen stove looked dead.

Dave took a piece of paper from the table and
handed it to me. I had never seen a cablegram before—but I knew at once that this was one. I read it.
I read it again. Then I began groping for a chair.
The kitchen floor was giving in under me. The cable
was short and to the point. COMING TO AMERICA,
BERNHARD WINKLER, it read. Among the mystical
symbols and figures on the head of the message I
saw the word Radautz. Father was coming. Radautz
was back in my life.

For a week we tried to find out whether the startling message was a hoax or the forebearer of tremendous events. It seemed all so incredible. Letters
had been exchanged regularly. We had reported our
progress, had written about our hopes and reassured
our dedication to the ultimate reunion of the family
here in America. But this all seemed far off. From
his own letters we had learned that Father had
changed his position since we had left; a certain
restlessness had come over his life and lately he had
not sounded quite as content and quite as supremely
sure of himself as we had known him to be in the
past. Never, however, had he even hinted at so
momentous a decision as he had now announced in
five forceful, awe-inspiring words: "Coming to America, Bernhard Winkler."

We took turns, Dave, Aunt Minnie and I, going to
all the shipping lines we knew, the North German
Lloyd, the Hamburg-Amerika Line, the British and

the Italian; and at last Dave came home with the news that a Bernhard Winkler was actually on board the S.S. *Kaiser Wilhelm,* a German vessel sailing from Cuxhaven and due here within a few days. I had no doubt but that the Bernhard Winkler on this ship was Father: nothing but a vessel named after a live emperor could be good enough to carry so majestic a man.

We wrote a note to brother Jack in Port Jervis, telling him the news. There was nothing else to do but to prepare oneself mentally and to go back to work. Arrivals of ships in those days were not known until the last minute. Any day, any hour the doorbell would ring. A growing feeling of excited anticipation and honest fear took hold of us.

The doorbell never rang. Instead, the mailman delivered a very anticlimactic note from the Immigration Office: Bernhard Winkler had arrived on the S.S. *Kaiser Wilhelm,* naming Max, Dave and Jack Winkler as his sons. "Will you please report to this office to make identification of said immigrant." I hurried down to Cooper Square to get the day off. Dave skipped all formalities. He let the Metropolitan Railroad Company drift by itself and joined me on the ferry to Ellis Island.

Father hadn't changed. His mustache—due maybe to the fact that he had traveled for so many days on the *Kaiser Wilhelm*—seemed even more belligerent and bristling with energy. He was still swinging a heavy walking stick, the same stick that had once terrorized five thousand lumberjacks, and although

at this moment he was nothing but "said immigrant"
looked just as determined to crush whatever resistance he might encounter on this side of the water.
His gray derby was brand new. His long dark overcoat had nothing of the rustic roughness of the
Carpathian Mountains. He was a new man, an *Amerikaner* already, an imposing figure of elegance and
poise.

The reunion with his sister Minnie whom he had
not seen in thirty years was an example of tearful
excitement from her and restrained condescension
on his part. Within an hour the apartment was swarm-
ing with people, relatives and friends I never knew
existed. They all had come to welcome Father. Where
had they all been when I had arrived? . . .

Everybody talked, everybody rushed around in
excitement, everybody brought gifts and refreshments. Everybody seemed to know everybody, except
that Dave and I knew nobody and nobody seemed
to care whether we did or not. Father, of course,
was the center of attention. He was really magnificently dressed and the way he spoke, acted and
looked made a deep impression on everybody. Here,
indeed, was a man of the world. Obviously he had
done a lot of reading about American history and
general conditions in the United States. He delivered
an impressive oration on what he knew to be the
best and only procedure to conduct a successful life
in the United States and disputed with brilliant elo-
quence anything anybody else would dare to say.
Soon everyone in his audience, people who mostly

had been here for many years if not for all their lives, were convinced that everything they had done so far was utterly foolish and completely wrong.

Later, after the guests had filed out, mumbling in admiration and bowing in respect, we sat around the table. Papa took off his coat. And, as we hadn't done since we had said good-by on the railroad station in Radautz, we all lighted up for a smoke.

Mama, Herman and Rose were fine, he reported, tersely.

"When are they coming here?"

"They will come as soon as we can afford to bring them here. How much money do we have?"

Dave and I got up and brought our bankbooks.

He looked at them and put them, without comment, in his pocket.

"Why isn't Jack here?" he asked.

We explained that there was no time to notify him.

"I will write him tomorrow. He has to come back to New York. We all must work together and save together. And now let's go to bed."

Dave and I went upstairs. Silently we went to bed. As during my first night here in this same room I couldn't sleep. I listened to the noises of the night that I had not noticed in a long time and wondered.

Early the next morning Papa was up in our room on the fifth floor.

"Sister Minnie told me last night that there is an empty four-room apartment in this house. I have decided to take it. It costs twenty-six dollars a month rent. I will buy furniture. You will give up your room here and we all will live together." We made no reply. It was time to go to work.

Within a few days life had changed. Our saving accounts had been transferred to two new accounts— one on the Dry Dock, one on the Germania Savings Bank—both under the name of Bernhard Winkler. On payday each week Papa received our pay envelope. He gave each of us one dollar pocket money per week. In addition to my salary I had, for the last few months, made five dollars a week by giving violin lessons at night—at fifty cents a lesson. I even had a doctor who paid me a dollar an hour for playing duets with him. Papa asked for and promptly received a list of my students. Every morning he collected my fees, but graciously agreed to let me retain ten cents carfare per lesson. I am still proud in reporting that I cheated him after all: I walked to most of my lessons and as for the spendthrift doctor I put him down for fifty cents only, thus netting a profit of sixty cents for every hour I played with him.

While all this was upsetting and not easy to stomach after a year of independence and toil we had to admit that father's sense of organization, iron discipline, and undisputed authority welded us into a splendid working team. He had rented the apartment, he had bought furniture—the most dilapidated compilation of odds and ends that could be found in a second, nay thirdhand furniture store on Avenue A —and even this sorry pile of junk he had bought on infinitesimal payments. Jack had defiantly written that he preferred to remain in Port Jervis. The next dawn saw father on a train. Come nightfall he returned not with Jack, who had slyly convinced him that he could be more useful to him in his present job, but with $214.00 in cash, the complete savings of our hapless brother. Father had also obtained a solemn pledge from him that he would send him eight dollars every week out of his salary from the railroad. It was magnificent. A week after he had arrived the old man had taken over the complete management and the exclusive control of the six hands and the three brains of his sons!

There was, however, still one little matter he had no part in—and that was Clara, my love. I had never mentioned her in my letters. How to tell him now, how to make him understand? One night I decided to talk the matter over with Dave.

"I am in the same boat," Dave said to my relieved surprise. "I, too, have been walking around in tight shoes for days. I didn't tell you yet, but I also have a girl. Her name is Ann. As long as we both are in the same boat let's talk to Dad together."

That sounded easy enough, but when we faced him the next morning over the breakfast table we felt like little boys who wanted to tell Papa that they had stolen apples. All our determination melted into air. We had stolen apples all right, but we didn't have the guts to confess. We went to work, brooding but silent.

A week passed. Saturday night Dave came home late. I knew that he had taken Ann to the movies.

I was sitting on needles as the hours passed on. Father kept on looking at the old clock.

"Where is Dave?"

"I don't know."

At last he went to bed. Dave sneaked in on tiptoe after midnight.

That night we bound ourselves by a solemn oath to talk to Father the next morning, and to take what was coming without losing our temper.

When we came down for breakfast Father was sitting at the table. He had the three bankbooks— Bernhard Winkler I, Bernhard Winkler II, Bernhard Winkler III—spread out before him and was engaged in serious calculations. Our skulls felt empty. For nineteen years they had been filled with absolute obedience. Our tongues just didn't function.

"What's the matter with you?" he suddenly asked.

He was an unbeaten master in reading our innermost thoughts.

"Oh, nothing."

"Sounds to me like plenty," he said, still looking at the bankbooks. *"Raus damit. Was ist los?"*

"Papa," I said, calling his name in a low tone, "you are right. We have something to tell you, something of great importance. It will not interfere with the plans we all have to bring Mother and the children here and to save enough to start in business. I am now nearly twenty years old." And, losing all the logical continuity of my carefully prepared speech, I blurted out in a humiliating short cut:

"And I don't expect to get married yet—maybe not until I am twenty-five or even older, really not, Papa."

Before I had ended he jumped to his feet, his cane in his right hand. For a moment I thought that he'd strike me. But he sat down again, as fast as he had come up. He was pale. The right half of his mustache was moving up and down with great rapidity as if his face was torn by spasms. I was terribly sorry for him. I suddenly loved him more than I ever loved him before. I didn't want to hurt him. He came from a different world, a world where every servant had kissed my mother's hand and every laborer bowed, hat in hand, at the sight of my father. He still lived in that world. He was its product. He couldn't help it. A year, a year of life in America, had changed me more than I had known until now. How could I make him understand?

"And what about you, Dave?" he said at last. "Are you just as stupid as he is?"

The collector of fares made no reply. He just bowed his head waiting for the blow to fall.

"I will not permit any acts of stupidity or disloyalty to interfere with my plans," Father said. He had gotten up and was now pacing the room. "I don't want to hear anything more about your girls. I warn you. You will not bring any girls in this house. If you do, I will throw them out. Do you understand German or have you also forgotten your mother tongue? Have you lost all respect for your parents?"

Before we had entered the room Dave and I had promised ourselves to take, in silence, what was coming. But now I couldn't restrain myself any more.

"Papa, you are wrong! We have not lost our respect for you. I promised you and Mother that I will all my life be loyal to you. But I also promised this girl to love her and I will do so for the rest of my life. This girl helped me and was my companion when I was all alone. She stuck to me when I was hungry and so poor that I didn't have a dime to take her to the movies. You have never seen her, you don't even know her name. Still you reject her. You even tell me you will throw her out of this house should I ever bring her here. *This house"*—I cried under tears—*"*wasn't it going to be *our house?"*

Father listened with great intensity. He remained silent for many minutes. So did we. Suddenly he rose, walked to the door and left the room.

Dave and I remained standing for a long time. We were simply frozen to the ground. When we sat down we had our faces in our hands, our eyes pinned to the floor.

We sat a long time.

"I wonder where he went," Dave said at last.

"Let's go and look for him."

We entered the kitchen. Father was leaning against a window. A man of fifty, looking like eighty. His face was terribly drawn. His eyes were closed.

"Papa," Dave said in a low voice, "are you sleeping?"

"No. I am not. But I am dreaming. I am trying to find myself in this strange and confusing dream. I wish Mama was here. If I only could talk to her. I wonder how long it will be till she will come."

"Send for her now, Papa," I said, taking him by the shoulders and looking at him with all the love and tenderness that was in me and with all the overwhelming pity I suddenly felt for him. "There is money enough in these three books to pay for the passage."

"But how will we live and eat?"

"Don't worry, you have three boys. We'll manage. We'll stick together."

He looked at us with a new and touching confidence. "Well, if you say so, I'll go to the steamship office tomorrow. Maybe Mama could be here in four weeks."

"Don't worry, Papa. Leave it to us."

He took the bankbooks again and began studying the figures. Then he put his hand in his pocket and took out a few coins.

"This is Sunday," he said. "Why don't you go to the movies? Here is a quarter for each of you. Maybe you want to take your girls along."

7.

June 19, 1908, was a happy day for all of us: a cablegram from the Hamburg-Amerika Line informed us that Mother and the children were on their way and that their ship was due in New York on the twenty-eighth. For nine days our talk, our dreams, every action centered around the long awaited moment when our family would again be united. Even Father seemed a changed man as he counted the hours. Never have I realized his deep devotion and love for my mother more than during these days, the longest nine days of our lives.

The day of arrival found us busy at dawn. The sun was just coming up and the clear beauty of the sky seemed to match the complete happiness of our hearts. We arrived on Ellis Island at seven in the morning although the steamship office had assured us the day before that the passengers would not pass inspection before 2 P.M.

And sure enough, at 1:30 in the afternoon they emerged. Little sister Rose spotted us before we discovered them and came rushing towards us, screaming with joy. Brother Herman grinned silently. Mother was intensely occupied, busy drying her tears, blowing her nose, smiling, crying, laughing, talking and keeping an eye on what seemed a mountain of bags, bundles, and valises. Soon she was flying from one pair of arms into the next. It took half an hour before she had made the rounds between Father, myself, Dave, and Jack who had come down to New York for the occasion. At last the seven of us got moving. Each of the boys had to carry two bundles and Mother kept on checking and counting them till, at last, exhausted but happy, the complicated caravan arrived at St. Mark's Place where Aunt Minnie had prepared the welcome table.

But Mother didn't sit down to enjoy her first meal in America. She walked around among her bundles and valises, counting them once more and then, at once, knelt down and began to unpack. We all understood. This was no ordinary baggage. Out of the bundles and boxes came Mother's whole life. There were sixteen large pillows, each at least three feet square, filled with the puffy feathers of thousands of geese she had raised and plucked for twenty-five years. Between the pillows she had packed plates and saucers, an old coffee grinder left to her by her mother, family pictures, a battered copper teapot, wooden spoons, a pair of candlesticks that had once been silver and were now black with age. There were hundreds of other things, big things and little things: they all had been part of our lives ever since we had learned to see and to walk and to eat. We had forgotten them and as they now emerged among the cold walls of an East Side flat in New York and among the sorry-looking pieces of secondhand American furniture that filled it, they brought a heart-warming touch of home into our hurried lives. Food would taste different from the plates of our childhood. The memories of tears and laughter, the good wind from the mountains, the smell of pine trees, stones thrown into a tall chimney, the cymbalo playing on the village green—all had been carried across the wide ocean with Mother's pillows, pictures and spoons.

. And there was still another magic and wonderful thing Mother had brought with her: a sack filled with thousands of buttons, large and small, buttons made of wood and buttons made of horn or mother-of-pearl, white buttons, green, red, black, rose ones, heavy and light, fancy and very common. As long as I could remember she had saved buttons, cutting them off every old piece of clothes, collecting them with a strange and tender passion. The sack had been known all over the village and nothing could make her happier than when a neighbor would come and ask to be permitted to fish for a button that would match the other buttons on her husband's paletot. If she would only search long enough and not lose patience she was sure to find what she was after in Mother's sack. I had played with the buttons when I was first crawling around the house. Their colors and shapes, the click they made when I made one of them jump in the air while pressing its rim with another button—they had all been part of my life. And now the buttons had come all the way from the Carpathian woods here to St. Mark's Place, a senseless and beautiful piece of what had once been home, childhood, happiness.

Mother, her bric-a-brac, her loving care, her

cooking, were back in the house, but its organization hadn't changed. Father remained, of course, in complete charge of everything. He left no doubt in the minds of any of us that a change in locality didn't mean a change in authority. His authority and unrestrained command over the management of the house and every one of its inhabitants had become even more accentuated: the energy that had once gone into the ruling of five thousand lumberjacks went now into a streamlined plan to make seven people save as much money as possible in the shortest possible time!

"Put wood on the fire while the wind is fanning it" was one of the many proverbs he used to recite with emphasis, and then continue to elaborate on such slightly stale morsels of wisdom by commenting that "nobody can figure out how the wind will be blowing around here with sons running around with girls at the age of twenty." In his eagerness to build the fire while the wind was still blowing he not only squeezed every dollar he could out of our pay envelopes and into the three bank accounts, he also skimmed a few percent off the food Mother was permitted to serve us. He knew every grocer, butcher, coal and ice dealer, every pushcart peddler within an area of thirty blocks. He had found out that he could buy three pounds of cow lungs for ten cents— enough to provide a family with food for an evening meal. He discovered stores that specialized in the sale of bread baked the day before and sold on the basis of "two breads for the price of one." There were pushcarts peddling canned goods no one had ever heard of and where you could buy a gallon of fruit juice (don't ask me what fruit and don't ask me what juice) for eleven cents—if you brought your own can. And if you had the patience, time and fortitude to cut out the worms you could carry home all the fruits and vegetables you wanted for fifteen cents—and the man gave you a basket into the bargain.

Mother's status remained what it always had been: she never handled money, never did any shopping, scarcely, if ever, left the house. Her cooking, deprived of all but the most primitive ingredients, frankly wasn't what I remembered it to be in the days when the mountain merchants supplied all her needs. Papa's provisions were a new and trying experience for Mother. She did her best but just couldn't always succeed and the strange dishes she had to concoct were consumed by the family either because we were too hungry to argue or just because the dishes were there and so was Papa. Every time Father brought home some unknown part of an animal, Mother would tell him: "Winkler"—she never called him by his first name—"Winkler, I feel again like a young bride when I used to put meat in a pot, add water, salt and a carrot and then leave it to God. Some thing had to come out—a soup, a goulash or a roast. I'll just try it again."

A year had scarcely passed since Mother, Herman and little Rose had arrived when a new and unexpected blow fell out of a sunny sky. Who, I ask, would ever consider himself an expert in the grocery business for no other reason than because he had been shopping for a year? Who, that is, but my father? As casually as if he wanted to comment on the weather outside he announced over the dinner table to a stunned family that he had decided to open a grocery store in the Bronx, that Dave was to quit his job with the Metropolitan Railroad Company to go in the business with him and that the family would move, within a week, to a thirty-two-dollar-a-month five-room apartment "with hot water and steam," on Simpson Avenue, a few minutes' walk from "my store."

I was petrified. Everything had been going so nicely. The family was united at last, the three accounts "Bernhard Winkler" had grown steadily, my own job had increased in scope and volume. I wasn't sweeping basement floors any more. The dreary rounds at the collating tables were a thing of the past: I was an order picker. An order picker in a music publishing house is something that doesn't exist in any other business and can only be compared for an outsider with the proverbial needle seeker in a haystack—although it is more complicated, more involved, and much more of a strain on your legs, arms and back muscles.

Through the dumb-waiter there descended a steady flow of slips listing music that was required by the clerks upstairs—piano pieces, songs, methods, violin solos, choral arrangements for every conceiv-

able combination of voices, orchestra music, a single
flute part for a band arrangement, vocal collections—
just anything. You had to know what all the marks
and numbers on the slips meant and then you had
to know where every one of these countless items was
stored. From the octavo bin for Men's Voices it was
a mile and a half through winding passages to the
song bins. A successful piece, such as Tobani's
"Hearts and Flowers," would be published as a song
in four different keys, as a choral number in at least
five different settings, as a piano solo (simplified)
and a piano solo (original), for piano four-hand and
six-hand and eight-hand, for zither and accordion,
for clarinet and brass. The Fischer catalogue contained at least 50,000 different items. 50,000 bins.
50,000 numbers. 50,000 chances to make a mistake.
And yet this sort of occupation had a strange fascination for me. At last I felt that I was working with
the music itself and the job forced me into an intimate acquaintance with thousands of selections that
filled the basement. Soon I knew many of them by
their numbers without having to look up the card
system that gave you a key to each individual title.
I loved to take the music out of the bins, to open
packages, to count out the required number of copies,
to make out the charge slip and send the whole pile
upstairs, on its way in the unknown world. At last
I had a first live contact with the very essentials of
my trade.

As my responsibilities grew so grew my feeling of
security. Slowly I forgot the haunting fear that I

would lose my job, a fear that had made "Jumbo" hurry and toil and take abuse and humiliation ever since I had set foot in the place. There was one incident that cured me definitely from this frightening obsession. A couple of kettledrums had been unloaded in the basement and one of the boys in the shipping department was just unwrapping them when I passed by. They looked beautiful, glittering in their polished brass, their skins dewy and new. I just couldn't resist the temptation to try them out. I took the sticks and let go with a thundering series of trills. But as I was ending my performance with a mighty beat, one of the drum heads split wide open. The drum suddenly fell into silence as if a shot had pierced a singer's heart. I was still standing there in speechless stupefaction when the boss, Mr. Carl Fischer, approached on one of his inspection tours through the underworld.

I knew the labyrinth of the basement better than he. Before he had uttered a word I had disappeared and I didn't stop till I had reached the sheltering shadows of Bin 57a, "Danube Waves," Octavo for Women's Voices. I was determined to starve rather than surrender.

"Where is the fellow that broke that drum?" I heard the boss's voice, slightly muffled by the distance I had put between his ire and myself. There was some commotion, the shuffling of feet. Silence.

"Who was that fellow?" the voice boomed again. This time there was a reply. "Oh, that was Jumbo." I thought I recognized Bebel's basso. Another voice

seemed to second the motion. Then silence again. I
waited for an hour before cautiously leaving my lair.

All afternoon I expected the blow to fall. But
nothing happened. As I left at night one of the book-
keepers called after me on Third Avenue.

"The old man was raving mad when he came upstairs," he reported. "He searched for half an hour
through the payroll for a man by the name of Jumbo.
When he gave up he seemed deeply disappointed.
'Must have been an expressman,' I heard him say.
'Too bad. That fellow certainly deserved to be
fired!'"

Yes, things were going fine all around. Dave was
still hanging on to his streetcars. Jack in Port Jervis
had increased his weekly contributions to ten dollars
and Father, who had never had a savings account
when he had five thousand lumberjacks, four horses,
a carriage, a footman and servants, had now three
savings accounts—one for each son. They remained
separated so that he would be able to determine at
a glance which of the boys contributed the most but
they were, of course, all in Father's name.

"What do you think I have been doing for nearly
a year, ever since Mama came over," he now declared.
"I have been studying the grocery business. I have
regularly bought in at least ten different stores. I know
all about it."

And while we all were sitting in silence around the
table, trying to think of a way to talk him out of it
and knowing already that there was none, he added
with unassailable finality: "Somebody told me that

new tenements, big enough to house a thousand families, are going up near the Intervale Avenue subway station. All these people will need food and all these families will buy groceries. In two weeks I will be in business. We will move next Tuesday."

And so we moved next Tuesday. Mother packed again her pillows and buttons and we bade good-by to Aunt Minnie and to the house on St. Mark's Place. I was almost sorry to leave its squalor, the dirty children with whom I had shared my first weeks and months in America, the people still sitting on the stoop. But there was no time to think or to shed a nostalgic tear. A truck with two tired-looking horses was waiting, we loaded what little there was to load and off we were—to the wide blue yonder of the lower Bronx.

Dave had bid a final adieu to the trolley cars of Manhattan. He was to be a partner in Father's grocery business. "You have been in the business before," Father told him, "you'll do fine." Dave had indeed a vast experience in the grocery trade—hadn't he started out life in the United States by helping hold the horse for a man who was peddling coffee, sugar and tea? The collector of fares was looking forward eagerly to a brilliant career as a businessman. There was a short flurry of rebellion when the painter put *Bernhard Winkler, Prop.* on the door of the new store—wasn't he, Dave, to be a partner? But his uncalled-for attempt of independence was stamped out vigorously. "Partner, Smartner," Papa said. "You do your work and let me do the worrying."

But if he did any worrying he never showed it. He was bubbling over with activity and optimism. For an entire week from dawn to dusk our new apartment was besieged by salesmen. The milk dealer had no sooner closed the door than the baker came in. Wholesalers of everything eatable descended like locusts on the place. Others had to sell paper bags, shelves, containers, flypaper, or door mats. Everyone had a lot of advice and a lot of merchandise and here they were sure to get rid of both. Early in the week one of them had sold Father the idea that "if you want the people to come to a new store you have to have things the old ones haven't got"—and now the idea that "my store" would be "different" had become his obsession. The traders soon found that out. Father listened, Father bought, Father went to the bank. He never mentioned any details to us but it was obvious that the three fat little savings accounts of Bernhard Winkler I, II and III lost weight at a frightening speed. But Papa was happy. Everything was fine. If anybody in the house did any worrying it was I who did it—but I kept my peace. What else could I do, anyway?

Finally the day of the grand opening arrived. The whole family had worked every night until four in the morning to get things in shape. Shelves and containers had gone up, and were now neatly stacked with merchandise. The floors had been swept. Woolworth had supplied pretty layers of bunting and even a bouquet of live flowers had arrived with best wishes from Aunt Minnie and could now be seen in one of mother's old vases between cornflakes and Rheingold. I had taken the day off and had put on my famous blue suit to act as the official greeter; Dave and Papa were behind the counter. The rest of the family stood outside, wondering why so many people passed the store and kept on walking.

And then the first customer came in. It was a small woman, poorly dressed, a bandana on her head.

Papa, of course, waited on her in person.

"What will it be, Madam?" he said. Mother, Herman and Rose came in the store. They stopped near the door, watching breathlessly. I turned on the smile of the greeter. Dave behind the counter began nervously polishing a tray of potato salad.

"I'd like some ketchup," the woman said.

"Dave—ketchup," Father snapped and Dave stopped polishing. From the shelf behind him he took a bottle of ketchup and handed it to the boss. Father put it in a bag.

"That will be eleven cents," he said.

"Let me see that bottle," the woman said.

Father, his mustache trembling slightly, took the bottle out of the bag and showed it to the woman.

"I don't want that ketchup," the woman said, handing the bottle back. "I want Gold Star Ketchup. The one with the big tomato on the label."

Father took the bottle and gave it back to Dave.

"Gold Star Ketchup," he said. "The one with the big tomato on the label."

Dave went back to the shelf. He looked at the bottles in the first row. He took them out and looked

at the bottles in the second row. He pulled the second
row out and looked again. The woman still waited.

Suddenly I saw Dave motion Papa to his corner.
A hurried conference of the two executives got under
way.

"Where is my ketchup?" the woman said.

"We don't have Gold Star Ketchup," Father replied in a firm voice. His mustache trembled still
more. I saw mother and the children turn and leave
the store in haste.

"We don't have Gold Star Ketchup," Father said
again. "What's wrong with this one?"

"Maybe nothing is wrong with it," the woman said.
"But I don't want it. We use Gold Star Ketchup."

"That's the trouble with you people!" Father said,
his face now purple. I forgot that I was a greeter and
stopped smiling. "You are taken in by advertisements
and you just do what they tell you to do. This here
ketchup . . ."

"I want Gold Star Ketchup," the woman said.

"But I tell you we haven't got it. *Himmeldonner-
wetter* why don't you listen to me. This here
ketchup . . ."

The woman looked nervously for the door. Then
she turned and began to run. I saw her keep on
running down the block and at last disappear in one
of the new tenement houses, one of the ones where a
thousand families were preparing themselves to buy
groceries, all friends and neighbors of Mrs. Gold Star.
I closed my eyes in desperation when a second customer came in. She asked for a can of peaches—Mag-

nolia Peaches. Every store carried Magnolia Peaches. We carried Eagle's. The customer didn't want Eagle's. She wanted Magnolia.

For the next weeks and months I saw little of the grocery store. I had little time to worry about it. I was only an occasional visitor on Sundays or dropped in early in the morning on my way to work. I saw some of the brands that were destined to "make this store different" disappear from the shelves and some better-known ones take their place but I never dared to ask what it had cost to make these changes and when I asked "partner" Dave he shrugged his shoulders—how could he know? Once in a while I heard that they had bought too much milk and butter and eggs and had to throw out half of it at the end of a day—there were no refrigerators in the store. And then, again, thinking that they had learned their lesson, they bought small quantities, only to see irate customers walk out after the timidly stocked supplies had been exhausted.

The neighborhood was full of people who had come from different countries and had kept their different eating habits. The cheese Father used to buy when he was a shopping apprentice on Delancy Street didn't appeal to the Italians who came in the store to ask for Bel Paese and never showed up again when they were offered Limburger instead. Germans didn't care for kosher wurst. *Beigels* were Greek to Greeks. Hungarians wanted salami, not *gefuellte fisch.* It was a great tragedy. Father became more and more irritated. He argued with the customers and he argued with the suppliers. Dave was helpless. He had become a very silent partner. He opened the store at 5:30 in the morning and closed it at 10:30 at night and after that he had no strength left to argue. He never received a salary. "Everything you need you can have right here in the store," Father decreed. Dave's name was still not on the door.

Everything seemed a conspiracy. One morning on my way to work I entered the store. Father was just raising the devil with a milk delivery man.

"Yesterday, when I opened the two cans you left here one was full of milk and the other one was just half full—with water! Water, water, just water—and you expect me to pay you."

The man didn't even stop to fight his case. He just turned around and began running towards a delivery truck that was parked a few houses down the street. I followed him. As he was climbing on the truck I heard him talk to his partner.

"What do you know," the delivery man said, "it's the third time since last week that they forgot to add the milk to the water. I told them a thousand times to put the milk in first and add the water later on. Oh, what the hell, let's go."

And they cantered down Simpson Street. Poor Papa—he surely had to fight the whole world.

I was foolish enough to tell him what I had heard, and it only served to strengthen his belief that everybody was out to cut his throat. To climax it all, one Sunday morning while I was in the store, a well-dressed man came in, walked over to Father and asked him most politely whether he could, please, change a ten spot for him.

"What does he want?" Father asked me.

"He wants you to change a ten-dollar bill."

Father opened the cash register, took out a five-dollar bill and placed it on the counter. He kept on searching only to discover that he couldn't change the ten dollars.

The stranger seemed unconcerned. "Maybe you can change a fiver," he said, extending a five-dollar bill.

"No," Father said, "I just haven't got it. What about some *leberwurst?*"

"Thanks, not today," the stranger said, put the five-dollar bill in his pocket and, lifting his hat graciously, left the store. And with him went Father's five-dollar bill.

None of us ever knew how much money the store took in, how much it owed, and how much was left on our savings accounts. Father did all the buying, fighting, rejecting, arguing, aggravating and what little selling there still was to do. The store never handled the same brand of bread, milk, cheese, butter or anything else for more than a few days before Father threw the delivery man out, asking him never to show his face again in "my store."

Every time I looked in, the shelves seemed not quite as full as they had been a few days before. Father obviously couldn't pay for new supplies any more. But I never had the heart to ask him. He was still busy in his store from the dark hours of the morning to the dark hours of the night. He looked old and tired. But he never let anybody share his troubles.

Ten and a half months after he had opened, the creditors finally caught up with him. The store had to close. What a dark day it was in Father's life! The shelves and containers, the few remaining cans and bottles, went on the auction block. Father sat there, with a stony white face, watching his dreams and hopes vanish before the pitiless voice of the auctioneer and the final blow of the hammer.

After it was over and the creditors had been paid, Mother had seven cans of peaches—Eagle's Peaches— on a shelf in her thirty-two-dollar-a-month apartment. That was all that was left of Father's grocery store.

The next morning, his face drawn, he gave us back our bankbooks. They contained, all three together, the amount of $13.47. The one marked Bernhard Winkler I, the one that had absorbed the fruits of my own labor for four and a quarter years, showed a balance of four dollars.

There I stood, on May 17, 1910, looking at my bankbook and wondering if such were the wages of perseverance and obligation to duty. Then I looked again at the little blue book. I couldn't help smiling. The balance, as I looked closer, didn't read $4.00. It read $4.01.

There was a penny left—a single solitary penny. Would it be another penny from heaven?

I put the book in my pocket and went downtown to work.

8.

The move to the Bronx, a full subway hour away from my job, from my violin pupils and from Clara, had been an added burden to my burdensome life. If I was to keep up the beloved and unchangeable habit of meeting my girl at 7:30 in the morning downtown, near our working places, I had to get up long before six; at eight work started in the dust and the darkness of the Fischer basement and didn't end before 6 P.M. But still the day wasn't over. Four evenings were taken up with violin lessons, and an occasional movie with Clara or a walk, or a talk on a park bench took care of the others. Seldom did I return home much before midnight. But no matter how late it was, my mother would still be sitting up, waiting with my supper. I gulped it down, half starved and completely exhausted, and fell on my bed.

Cheap cuts of meat and cow lung goulash were again back on our menu. Cow lung *hache* might be a fine dish if you take it as an appetizer, nicely dressed up with onions, and then follow it up with a plate of soup *du jour*, a filet mignon or two, a frozen eclair maybe, or a pear in wine, and a demitasse. But it has a very different effect on you if you devour it in large quantities, after a fifteen-hour day.

My luncheons, too, were something to remember.

They were mostly taken at a free-lunch counter where the purchase of a glass of beer would give you access to a selection of dishes—herring, salami, secondhand cheese—that in these more enlightened days would land the proprietor of the place behind the bars of justice within twenty-four hours. If I didn't partake of one of these feasts I lunched on a sandwich where one could never guess what was between the two slices of stale bread and what had been smeared on whatever was between them to make it taste like something it wasn't.

Slowly the pitiless abuse my body had taken for the past few years began to show its effects. I developed a dull pain at the end of my breastbone where the ribs spread out. It increased in intensity. Soon attacks of tormenting pain recurred with clocklike regularity, mostly in the afternoon. I fought them with all my energy. At last I had to see a doctor.

The doctor occupied a tiny office just around the corner from our apartment on Simpson Street. As I entered, the waiting room was packed with people. It was late in the day. The people looked pale, very tired, very poor. Like myself, they all crowded their visit into this hour—the hour after a full working day. Nobody spoke. Nobody looked at one of the old magazines, thrown sloppily on a table in a corner. They all just sat, motionless, waiting their turn.

Every two minutes the door to the doctor's office was thrown open, a patient came out and the doctor, a small, elderly man in shirtsleeves, said "Next" in an impatient, irritated voice. One of the silent shadows got up, crossed the room in haste as if called in by an investigating policeman to be questioned on some terrible accusation and the doctor shut the door again.

At last it was my turn. Before I could say a word the doctor—he had thin gray hair and a little dirty-yellow mustache—began firing questions at me in a monotonous voice. He never waited for or listened to any of my answers. At last he placed his right ear on my left shoulder and listened for a second or two. Suddenly he pushed his fist in my stomach. I yelled out in pain. He listened again. A strong smell of ether, alcohol and garlic emanated from him. I felt faint.

"There is nothing the matter with you," the doctor said. "You eat too much. Eat less. One dollar, please."

He pushed open the door, shouted "Next" and I saw an old woman get up and cross the room. Before the door had been closed I already heard him firing away at her with his barrage of questions.

I ate less, reducing the little I had eaten before to almost nothing. The pains increased. When I was hungry my stomach felt like a ten-story house in hell with a special tormenting department on every floor. I endured it for three months. Then Clara made me see another doctor. This one lived downtown, on the East Side. It made me feel good to see my old hunting grounds again, St. Mark's Place and Avenue B—it was like home-coming. And the doctor, too, was nice. He took much more time with me, at least three minutes.

"There is nothing the matter with you," he told me

at last, cheerfully. "You just don't eat enough. Eat more. But don't eat fat. One dollar fifty, please."

So far I had carefully avoided telling my mother about my condition. I knew her too well. But now, if I was to follow the cheerful doc's advice not to eat fat, I had to take her into my confidence. The next day the lung *hache* and all the other strange dishes she had been forced to concoct under the iron rules of the house had disappeared from my midnight snacks. Mother had made breakfast for the family at 5:30 in the morning, she had looked after Rose and made lunch and dinner for Father and Dave and Herman at different times of the day—and she was still waiting patiently for me while everybody else was long asleep, with a bowl of rice, a farina pudding, a couple of eggs gently reposing on soft creamed spinach—anything she could think of to make me eat, breaking into tears when I was too tired or too much shaken by the ever-increasing pains to touch her food.

I didn't eat fat. For some time I thought that my health was improving. Then a sudden attack almost threw me off one of the sliding ladders in the Fischer basement. I followed the advice of one of my fellow workers of the basement brigade and went over to 24th Street to see Doctor Schmeidler.

The doctor, at first, didn't seem any different from his predecessors. His waiting room was crowded with working people. But then I saw, to my amazement, that the wall of the room was covered with pictures of musicians—and as I looked closer they were all violinists—Paganini, Joachim, Ysaÿe, Heifetz and a small child—Mischa Elman. There was Fritz Kreisler whom I had seen many times from my secret observation post behind the pillar near the orchestra department. There was the great Leopold Auer. What was going on here?

I had to know. After he had finished his recitation of questions—I knew all about them by now and could answer them without listening to any of them —I said:

"I admired your pictures, Doc. How come you have a picture of Heifetz in your waiting room?"

Doctor Schmeidler looked up in amazement. It was obvious at once that he was highly pleased and completely surprised by the fact that any of his patients had observed his musical gallery.

"Did you ever hear him play?" he asked, looking at me eagerly.

"No," I said. "But I know him."

The doctor jumped off his seat.

"You know Heifetz?" he cried. "My God, who are you?"

I knew at once that I had said the wrong thing. But how could I retreat?

"I am a music publisher," I said. "Well, I mean, I work in a music publishing house. We are Heifetz' publishers."

"That is marvelous!" the doctor said. "You are just the man I have been looking for. Sit down, please, make yourself comfortable."

On his desk I saw the picture of a small boy, holding a violin that seemed much too large and a bow that was definitely too long for his small hands.

The doctor took the photo. "This is Reuben," he said. "Reuben is a wonderful fiddler. The other day he played the Largo by Handel at my sister-in-law's anniversary—I am telling you, that kid is an artist. All he needs is a break. Now if you will ask Heifetz to listen to him, that's all the kid needs. I'll send him down to the store to play for you."

"Doc, now listen, I don't think . . ."

"But you haven't heard him yet. Just wait till you hear him. I am telling you that kid . . ."

"But really, look, you don't understand, I . . ."

"Don't worry, don't worry, we will take care of you. Now you just make Heifetz listen to the kid, I am telling you . . ."

I gave up. Timidly I asked the doctor what to do about my stomach. But he wasn't interested any more.

"You know, when I read in the papers about all these artists, it just burns me up. Now Reuben, I am telling you—oh, yes, your stomach troubles you. Don't worry. You just work too hard. Take it easy. Go to the beach. Relax. Now you just wait till you hear Reuben. I'll send him down first thing in the morning. Two dollars, please."

Slowly my sufferings began to place a stamp of agony on my face. I was always tired. My cheeks felt hot. People didn't say "Good morning" when they saw me—they greeted me, instead, with an encouraging "My, you look sick," or a cheerful "Whatsthematterwithyou—why don't you see a doctor?" And then they began giving me advice.

"You have to drink more water—very cold water, just as much as you can get down," people said.

"I know a fellow who had exactly your trouble. My, it almost killed him. He looked just as awful as you do. Know what he did? The man bought himself a bicycle. You should see him today. Nothing wrong with him any more. All he needed was exercise."

"Drink milk, hot milk, as hot as you can swallow it. Abe Minkowitz . . . "

"Drink cold milk."

"Lime Water."

"Sugar."

"Sugar, I'm telling you, sugar is poison."

"Salt."

"Never use salt."

I listened to stories about people who were cured and I listened to stories about people who had died, died very painfully and after a long and protracted suffering—"poor devil, he had the same symptoms you have and there was just nothing anybody could do for him."

I probably survived because of my never-swerving devotion to work and duty, and my unbreakable determination to hang on. Every time the pains were on the verge of overpowering me I would think of the happy years I had mapped out for Clara and myself. I never was absent from my job for a single day. I gave every lesson on schedule. Day and night I waged a never-ceasing battle with myself.

I thought that I was the winner. I didn't know that I was living on borrowed time.

I thought that by the sheer power of determination I could defeat the invisible monster within myself.

I paid very dearly for my foolishness later in life.

One day, in the autumn of 1911, I was sitting on a bench in Cooper Square, across the street from the Fischer store, trying to nibble down a sandwich. An old man was sitting next to me. He watched me eat.

"You are not feeling well?" he suddenly asked in a soft, gentle voice. I was immediately attracted by him. He was poorly but very neatly dressed. In his lapel he had a small white carnation. His hat, shiny with age, was carefully brushed. He was clean-shaven. His collar, slightly frayed, was white.

I was very tired of people who asked me about my looks. I had heard too much about it lately. My first impulse was to get up and just walk away. But I hadn't the heart to hurt the old man. I began talking to him. I suddenly felt an urge to tell him all about my troubles. I did. I spoke about my visits to the doctors, how I had given up all hope of being cured by any of them, about the terrible strain I was living under. I spoke about my mother, about my work, about the constant battle for survival and I also spoke about my fear—a fear that I had scarcely admitted to myself and that I now, suddenly, heard myself reveal to a perfect stranger—the fear that I would lose that battle.

"I know a lot about what ails you," the old man said. He had never interrupted me. He had scarcely moved. He seemed far away, smiling at I didn't know what. "I myself," he added, "have been ill for the greater part of my life."

I looked at him. He didn't look ill. He looked old and poor, but the more I looked at his face the more it struck me as the face of a happy man.

"What is your name?" I asked him.

"Just call me Doctor," the old man said. "It reminds me of the days when I really was a doctor."

"What would you prescribe for me, Doctor?" I said, smiling myself in his heart-warming presence. I felt no pain. The midday sun was gentle.

He made no reply. "Yes," he said instead, "I was a sick man, a discouraged man for almost fifty years. I suffered, just as you. I had nervous breakdowns. I hated people. Everything and everybody annoyed me.

"But I was a doctor," he continued after a little while. "I didn't have to describe my pains to another quack. I felt them, I had them, and I worked on them myself. I tried everything I knew of, everything science had to offer. I was helpless and confused. Sometimes I looked at my medicine chest—there, within my grip were powders that would end it all, quickly, painlessly. I was longing for a rest, believe me."

He stopped and looked at me. Did he know that I, too, had sometimes thought about a way that would end all my troubles once and for all? . . . He didn't say. He just stopped for a moment and watched me. Then he spoke again.

"Just when I thought I couldn't take it any more," the old doctor continued, "I met a young minister. He had recently moved into our neighborhood. We soon began to go for an occasional walk together. I told him about my life and my troubles. 'What is the use of living?' I once cried out. 'What hope is there?'

"The young minister looked at me with gentle eyes. 'You are a doctor,' he said, 'a learned man, a man of science. But even you have stood at many a sickbed where all your science didn't prevail. You, too, have read about people stranded in midocean, spending days on a life raft, thirsty, starving, burned to death by the sun. There was no appeal to science, and reason, and logic. These people looked up at the stars at night and saw the Southern Cross, and the Dipper and the brilliant Orion—they saw rainbows during the day and clouds and the sun sinking into the tremendous sea. Science had lost all its significance to them. They looked up into the sky. And they found a strength and consolation in their prayers that none of them could explain after they had been picked up and put in a nice comfortable bed and given injections and pills and all the care of science.

" 'You don't have to be on a lonely raft in the Pacific to need God. You need him here, today, any time when all your knowledge and all your medicine chests can't help any more. Give him a chance. Believe. You'll be all right.' "

The big clock of Cooper Union approached dan-

gerously close to our parting hour. I got up. The old
man smilingly extended his hand.

"I'll see you again," he said. "I always sit here during the warm hours of the day. Pay me another visit."

But I never saw him again. For many days I passed
the bench, looking for him. He was never there.

I went back to work that day, humming a tune,
carrying my head high and walking briskly. When
I came down into the basement, Hoffmann looked at
me with amazed eyes.

"Whatsthematterwithyou?" he said. "Why, you
look fine."

I felt myself smiling as I walked over to the order
basket to pick up an order that called for one copy
each of seventy-three different octavo numbers.

An hour later Hoffmann came down from the upstairs offices in great excitement.

"Mr. Walter Fischer wants to see you immediately," he said. I had completed a pile of fifty-nine
octavos. I dropped it on the floor, put on my jacket
and went upstairs.

The call to Walter S. Fischer's office didn't frighten
me. He was one of the three sons of the boss who as
their father began to grow older had gradually taken
over the management of various branches of the business. Carl Jr. was in charge of instruments. George
handled the piano department. I saw little of them
and scarcely knew them. But Walter, in charge of
the publishing end of Carl Fischer's, had for quite
some time been my immediate superior. And while

there was, of course, very little contact between the
son of the owner and an order filer in the basement,
I had developed a deep affection and sincere admiration for him.

Among the many rude, cynical, egoistic men I had
been working with, young Walter Fischer had been a
consoling exception. As I walked up the stairs to his
office I remembered a little incident that had happened in my very early days of floor sweeping and
toilet cleaning here at Fischer's; it meant so little now
as I thought of it, and yet it had done more than anything else I could remember to help me survive the
last four years. I had been sweeping the floor between
the narrow bins for a good part of the morning when
Walter Fischer passed me. He looked at me, smiled
with his clear eyes, and his clear eyes and his friendly
face greeted me with a cheery good morning.

I was deeply touched. I almost cried. Here was I,
a greenhorn, sweeping floors among people who
would hold their noses when I passed them—and the
son of the owner of this great house bade me a
friendly good morning! Suddenly I felt that I was
somebody, a human being, accepted in spite of my
humble situation as a fellow man, an equal among
equals. This could never have happened in the country where I had come from, a country where the
floor sweepers waited, hat in hand, while the boss's
son passed them. This was different. Suddenly I
didn't mind Bebel and Goetz and Hoffmann with all
their contempt and abuse any more. These men
weren't America. Walter Fischer greeting a dirty

little floor-sweeping nobody with a friendly good morning—he was America. I had never forgotten his friendly words of welcome and acceptance. They had become for me a symbol of my new country and they comforted me in the dark hours of defeat and despair. Much later, in an even more crucial moment of my life, I would again have occasion to remember the little incident and the friendly eyes and kindly word of Walter Fischer who again was to step forward and extend a helping hand. He wouldn't be my boss any more. He would be my friend. But this was still far away, in the distant mist of the future. . . .

As I entered Walter Fischer's office he asked me to sit down. With a few words he told me that I had been promoted from the basement to the main floor. I was to be in charge of the stock for the orchestra and band department. At first I didn't trust my ears. Then I got up from my chair, stammered a confused "Thank you" and went back downstairs.

Slowly I began to comprehend what had happened. What I had learned down among the bins, staggering under back-breaking loads of music, rotating endlessly around the collating tables, picking out orders in daily tormenting fights with my revolting stomach—it all had not been in vain.

The basement brigade, when I told them the news, seemed stunned. I tried hard not to show my elation. I knew that all these men were unhappy because they hated their jobs. They had long since lost the capacity to free themselves from the monotonous feeling of resignation that had taken hold of them. Many times

we had debated—they laughing at my ambition, my
haste, my obsession to do my job, any job, right, my
indestructible belief that hard work and devotion to
duty would at last be rewarded. They blamed the
boss, they blamed Hoffmann, they blamed everybody
and everything but themselves. I had long since
given up debating with them. This, the music business, I knew was the one thing I was beginning to
learn. If I wanted to get out of the cellar I had to
learn enough to know some of the things that weren't
done in the cellar. This had been my simple philosophy. "You'll never succeed," Bebel had said. "Look
at me. I have been here sixteen years. And I'll be here
for the rest of my life."

"You'll never succeed." I had never believed him.
And now I had succeeded.

The next morning for the first time since I had entered the doors of Carl Fischer's I did not walk down
the stairs. I went over to the orchestra counter. I said
"Good morning" to Mr. Louis Werner, the manager of
the department. Then I went to the rear to hang up
my coat and hat in one of the four wooden lockers
reserved for the clerks on the floor.

I opened the door of the first locker and hung up
my clothes. Five seconds later they were lying in the
dust.

"Your junk belongs in the last locker," shouted
Harry Ruppel, one of my new colleagues.

I didn't reply. I picked up my hat and my coat,
dusted them off and put them in locker No. 4.

I had learned to take my time.

My hat and my coat still belonged in the last locker.

It didn't matter.

All that mattered was that I was here—upstairs!

9.

After four years in the dungeons, light at last, air, the first timid dawn of liberty!

The hollow voices from the dumb-waiters were silenced at last. Now I was doing the dumb-waiter shouting myself, waiting proudly for the answer from below. "Ten copies of 'Semper Fidelis,'" I called out —and "Ten copies coming up" the eager echo answered. A minute later a buzz, a click, and there were the ten copies, nicely stacked in a corner of the little elevator. I took them out, lovingly, and put them away.

It was my job to see to it that orchestra and band music from every publisher in the country and in the whole world would always be on hand in sufficient quantities, properly stored, easily accessible. I had to order enough supplies at the right time, had to see to it that my bins, thousands of them, were never too empty or too full. I had to know what would sell and what wouldn't, I had to be sure not to overbuy or to be stuck with piles of worthless junk.

It was a great feeling to be able at last to use the knowledge I had acquired in the tedious years downstairs. For the first time I was in touch with the outside world. I did not have to hide behind pillars any more when celebrated artists, bandleaders and orchestra conductors came into the store. I met many of them, spoke to them, began to understand their problems. I learned every day and every hour. Like a sponge, I took in knowledge and experience through every pore.

From day to day I felt myself standing on firmer ground. A new unknown feeling of security began to take hold of me. I had never gone to college, never acquired a degree. But now I began to learn something that no title, no beautifully printed diploma could ever give me: the sound knowledge of a given job, experience in a profession that I had chosen by accident and that now began to become a solid part of myself. I walked easier. The last vestiges of the haunting fear of losing my job began to disappear. Even my physical pains began to diminish in a joyful feeling of assurance that warmed body and soul.

Every morning I delved into my work with eager anticipation. Down in the cellar I had learned to know every number in the Fischer catalogue. Now I had to extend my knowledge to everything that was printed anywhere in the world. New titles, as they came in, were played to us by a staff pianist—it wasn't enough for us to know the name of a piece, we had to know its character and general grade of difficulty. It was a thorough schooling and the time wasn't too far away when it would yield me rich and unexpected fruit.

I began to reorganize everything within my domain. I wrote out thousands of little cards, indicating where every one of these innumerable items was to be found, giving information on subtitles, on individual movements of any composition, on the publisher, the key, on different arrangements of the same selection, on prices. Louis Werner, the head of the department, didn't say much. He let me drift along with the patient resignation of an old-timer who had seen many new brooms break out in violent action, only to see them settle down after a little while to the dreary routine that distinguished a pleasant employee from a hatefully alert troublemaker. I was a great disappointment to him: I refused to settle down.

Werner was quite a character. He was a man in his late forties who had been with the house of Fischer for no less than thirty-four years. He seemed to blend perfectly with the dark wood of the old bins, with the dust and the stale smell of the store. He walked slowly, talked slowly, thought slowly. He never got excited. Thirty-four years of continued service had dehydrated him. He was never sick, he was never drunk, he never talked about anything but orchestra and band music. But in his field Werner was a walking encyclopedia. I had never seen anything like him before. He would never consult a list or a catalogue in order to produce even the oddest bit of information unfailingly. The card system I was working on so painstakingly was to him only a matter of disdain and utter indifference.

You could ask him about a Waltz published in Vienna thirty years ago or about a German *Militaermarsch*, popular at the time of Frederick the Great, you could search for information on an Italian Tarantella or a Kentucky Mountain Ballad: Louis Werner would recite without a moment's hesitation the name of the composer, the year and place of publication, the form and the orchestration, and—whether you asked for it or not—the price of a complete copy and the price of a single piccolo part.

Here, however, his world seemed to end. It was impossible to talk to him about anything but band and orchestra music. Did he have a house? A dozen or two children? A dark-eyed mistress? Did he play the horses, vote for a political candidate, collect butterflies? Nobody knew. The only indication we had that there was at least something human in Louis Werner was the fact that every Saturday when he received his pay envelope we would see him go to a dark corner, open the envelope with utmost care, erase the amount that was written inside the flap, fill in a different figure and take out some of the contents before closing it again. This he did for many years, Saturday after Saturday, stealing a dollar or maybe just a few coins from nobody knew whom for some unknown purpose.

Why, we never found out. Werner never talked anything but titles, prices and numbers. Once in a while the fellows on the floor tried to strike up a conversation with him but he only gave them a blank look. If they tried to make him listen to their perpetual stories and jokes, the dreary make-believe world of every salesman, he would sit there with an irritated and tired grimace on his thin lips, as if nothing could penetrate a mind that for thirty-four years had surrounded itself with the facts and figures of an empty paper world.

"Werner," they would say, "know the one about the specialist who asked a man to leave his brain with him?" The story had been told a dozen times but Werner made no sign of acknowledgment.

"Well," they would continue, "the specialist told this man that his brain needed cleaning and some general repairs. Would he please call for it in a week? Months passed, the man didn't call for his brain. One day the specialist met him in the street.

" 'Why don't you call for your brain?' the specialist asked. 'It's all in order now.'

" 'Thanks a lot,' the fellow replied, 'but I don't need it any more. I am now manager of an orchestra department.' "

Werner just turned away and walked over to a clerk who was waiting to ask him what *Esclarmonde* was.

"It's an opera by Massenet, published in 1889 by Heugel in Paris. We carry a Phantasy for Orchestra and a March, price seventy-five cents each, you'll find it in Bin 349, Shelf 7c. Be careful when you take it out, the wrapper is slightly torn."

Poor Werner! He was always faced by events that seemed just beyond his powers of mental digestion. I will never forget the day—a Saturday afternoon, the busiest hour in the store—when my twin brother Dave decided to pay me a visit to see for himself how I was doing in my elevated position.

There had been trouble enough with Dave in the

past. Time had not changed our fatal similarity. Once when I passed by accident the coffee and tea peddler Dave was working for, the man had jumped off his wagon and begun yelling at me for "quitting the job in the middle of the day and walking around in a derby." Another time on my way to work I walked past a streetcar, right in front of the two horses hitched to the car.

"Hey you, Wink!" a stentorian voice began to holler. "What are you doing in front of my horses? Get back on the car and take that silly hat off your silly head." I stared at the man in complete bewilderment. The next moment he jumped off the car, grabbed my arm and started to hurl a flow of invective at me, most of which, fortunately, I didn't understand.

"Let go!" I yelled. "I'm not your conductor."

He began shaking me. "Like hell you're not. You can't quit in the middle of the day. There are laws in this country. I'll get a cop." And he began screaming at the top of his lungs.

In the meantime the streetcar, still standing peacefully in the midst of 28th Street, had created a formidable traffic snarl. People, hundreds it seemed to me, had gathered around us. The man tried to pull me on his car. I was resisting forcefully when a cop finally broke through the barrier of sidewalk superintendents.

"What's going on here?" he demanded. But before anybody could say a word I felt the driver's grip loosen and saw his jaw sag as if something had suddenly hit him. And something had. There, through

the gap made by the cop, came Dave, the collector
of fares, pushing his way through the crowd.

"What's the matter, Joe?" he said. "What's holding
you up?"

Then Dave saw me. He knew at once what had
happened.

"It's all right, officer," he said, patting the startled
cop on the back. Then he took hold of Joe who was
still turning his head from Dave to me and from me
back to Dave.

"Let's go, Joe," Dave said. "I'll tell you all about it
after we get rid of the rush load. Good-by, Max, see
you later."

The last I saw was Joe taking up the reins again
and calling to his horses to giddap, a wild and dangerous look in his eyes.

These things happened to us all the time. And now
Dave was strolling into the Fischer store, walking
over to the orchestra department to look for me. After the grocery debacle he had meekly made his
peace with the Metropolitan Railway Company. He
was again wearing their cap and uniform.

He looked for me but I wasn't there. Just about a
minute earlier I had been called down to the basement where one of the dungeon slaves had trouble
finding the Mandolin parts of the *Fledermaus* Overture. I had motioned to Werner, pointing my left
thumb downstairs—meaning in the orchestra department's vernacular "I'll be downstairs for a while"—
and left on my mission. No sooner had I disappeared
than Conductor Dave walked in!

Werner saw him approach. His mind, so thoroughly out of touch with anything but the protected routine of his work, must have received a terrible shock. At first he didn't say a thing. He just stood there, staring at Dave, trying to apprehend what seemed so utterly unapprehendable.

"Don't play games here in the store, on a Saturday afternoon," he said at last. "Please don't. This is terrible. You just went down the stairs. . . . "

Dave, of course, immediately knew what was the matter.

"Downstairs? What are you talking about?" he said jauntily.

"Come on now, Winkler," Werner stammered, "you are mad. My God, if Mr. Fischer finds you here in this masquerade . . . "

"My dear man," Dave said, "I never saw you in my life. I came here to see my brother."

As if all the pent-up passion of thirty-four years were suddenly coming to the surface, Werner exploded.

"Get out of here!" he cried. "Take that silly cap off, go back to work or I'll fire you myself."

At that moment I came back into the store. I heard Werner's screams, saw his face purple—a face that I had never seen ruffled by even the slightest emotion! And then I saw Dave.

I walked over, gently, and touched poor Werner's sleeve. He looked at me for a short instant. Then he sat down, very quietly. He just shook his head once or twice. His face resumed its old color. The explosion had passed. He looked as if for the next thirty-four years nothing again would ever matter but the Potpourri from Massenet's *Esclarmonde*.

"I told you that I was here to see my brother," Dave said. But Werner didn't hear him any more. He was safely back in the world of publication dates and French Horns.

I learned a lot from Louis Werner, but I also learned through him how dangerous it was to become nothing but a specialist. With all his knowledge he seemed to me only a duplication of my ex-fellows of the basement brigade, a man running around in circles, chained to his own limited knowledge, shut off from the light of the day and the fresh air of life. I wasn't to be trapped like him.

Driven by my will to go ahead, never to stand still, I began to make suggestions to Werner, to the clerks, to Mr. Walter Fischer himself. All told I must have been quite a nuisance. Soon, however, fate looked after me again and taught me a friendly lesson.

One bright morning I received an order from a music dealer in a little town in the state of Iowa asking for a copy of Franz Liszt's *Les Preludes* arranged for military band. I went to my famous card system and when I couldn't find it there I asked Werner.

"There ain't no such animal," Werner said without hesitation and when he said so I knew that there wasn't a band arrangement of *Les Preludes* published in the whole wide world.

I mentioned it to Mr. Fischer.

"We should publish *Les Preludes* for band," I said. "We are getting requests for it. I think it would be a magnificent selection for band."

"How many requests did you get?"

"Well," I said, slowing down a little, "so far only one. But I think..."

Mr. Fischer just looked at me, shrugged his shoulders and walked away.

The next morning two more requests for a band arrangement of *Les Preludes* came in, one from Chicago, one from St. Louis. A week later I had one from San Francisco, one from Boston, four from New York. I was delighted. I had taken my first stab at publishing, the boss had snubbed me and now, look who was right and look who was wrong!

Another week or two passed and I had on my desk a carefully guarded stack of thirty-seven orders for *Les Preludes.*

The next time Mr. Fischer passed my counter I took them out, spread them out attractively and suggested once more that Fischer's publish the selection.

"Winkler," Mr. Fischer said, "I think I owe you an apology. This sounds like a fine idea. Thanks. We'll publish the number right way."

A few months later a thick blue wrapper containing the newly published band arrangement of *Les Preludes* was on my counter. I felt fine. It was a beautiful edition and I knew that it had cost a lot of money to prepare and to print. But what did it matter? I took my thirty-seven orders and filled every one of them the same afternoon, at ten dollars a piece.

Twelve days later thirty-six copies had come back. What had happened? Slowly I pieced the terrible story together. A bandmaster in Iowa had gone to his local music dealer and asked for a band arrangement of *Les Preludes*. The dealer didn't have it, told the customer so and wrote to Carl Fischer for a copy. But the customer was in a hurry. He went home and wrote thirty-six letters to music dealers all over the country, and the thirty-six dealers all over the country wrote to Fischer's! And now the dealer in Iowa had sold a copy to the lunatic, the one single copy that had started all this, and the other thirty-six had had no use for it and had returned it. "Will you please credit my account," the thirty-six dealers wrote, "sorry, thank you for your attention, sincerely yours."

Thus ended my first publishing venture. Mr. Walter Fischer, kind man and perfect gentleman that he was, never mentioned the name of Liszt in my presence again. One of these days I have to go down to Carl Fischer's and find out how many copies of the original edition of *Les Preludes* for band they still carry in stock....

10.

1912 was the beginning of the greatest and most prosperous era in the history of the American amusement industry. Scores of theaters played on Broadway. Victor Herbert was at the peak of his fame. Irving Berlin had entered the Hall of Glory. Vaudeville branched out mightily throughout the country. Big chains such as Fox or Loew's began to hire vaudeville acts with guarantees that would extend to as much as a hundred and four weeks of continuous employment.

All this had tremendous repercussions on the world of music publishing and soon the mighty waves of excitement and prosperity reached the band and orchestra counter in the Fischer store. We began to sell ever-increasing, unheard-of amounts of waltzes and songs, of potpourris and marches, of overtures and interludes. Orchestra arrangements of the popular songs of the day arrived from the printers in staggering quantities and were rapidly disposed of.

What radio has become to the song of today, Broadway and Vaudeville were to the tunes of yesterday. Singers who went on a two-year tour on the Vaudeville circuit became a most valuable asset to a composer and his publisher: they were the ideal pluggers for a song and they soon knew it and began to act accordingly. The stars of Vaudeville began to collect higher and higher fees from the publishers for promoting their songs. After a while every trumpet player, singer, barbershop quartet, or accordionist put out an eager hand before he would touch any piece of music. To buy—or rather not to buy—music, had almost become a point of honor for this tremendous army of professional musicians.

Sometimes things threatened to get out of control. I still remember a mustached gentleman who came to my counter one bright afternoon and asked for a copy of the "Star-Spangled Banner." I handed him the music. He thanked me politely, turned around and started on his way out.

"Thirty-eight cents, please," I called after him. "You forgot to pay for the music."

"Me pay for music?" he replied with a furious look. "I play in Fox Circuit. I give song a big plug."

Nothing that happened in the rapidly expanding world of musical comedies, operettas and vaudeville was comparable, however, to the breath-taking development of the silent movies. The giants of the film and amusement industry known to the present generation were beginners then but already they had made their mark on an industry that suddenly changed the whole country. William Fox, Sam Goldwyn, Louis Selznick, began to produce films on a large scale in Hollywood. Big movie theaters went up not only in New York but by the hundreds and thousands in every town and village. This was of tremendous consequence to the music business: the film, silent and dead on the screen, needed music to bring it to life.

"On the silent screen music must take the place of the spoken word." This had become one of the credos of the film industry. Huge theater orchestras were hired to play in the movie palaces of the big cities and smaller ensembles, trios, or simply a pianist or an organist entered the employ of movie theaters by the thousands in towns and villages. Their musical situation, however, was desperate.

Only in a few isolated places in the big cities was any effort made to co-ordinate the goings-on on the screen with the events in the musical pit. Thousands of musicians never had a chance to see a picture before they were called to play music for it! There they were sitting in the dark, watching the screen, trying to follow the rapidly unfolding events with their music: sad music, funny music, slow music, sinister, agitated, stormy, dramatic, funereal, wedding, pursuit music. They had to improvise, playing whatever repertoire came to their worried minds or whatever they made up themselves on the spur of a short moment. It was a terrible predicament—and so, usually, were the results.

On a lovely day in the spring I took Clara to one of the small movie houses that had begun to spring up all over town. The picture was one of the superb spectacles of the day. It was called *War Brides* and featured the exotic Nazimova in the role of a peasant woman in pregnancy. The ruling king of the mystical country where Nazimova was living with her family

passed through her village. It was a pompous parade
of uniforms and horses. As the king passed, Nazimova
threw herself in front of him, her hands raised to
heaven. She said—no, she didn't say anything but the
title on the screen announced, "If you will not give
us women the right to vote for or against war I shall
not bear a child for such a country."

The king just moved on. Nazimova drew a dagger
and killed herself.

The pianist so far had done all right. But I scarcely
believed my ears when no sooner had Nazimova ex-
haled her last breath to the heartbreaking sobs of her
people than the man began to play the old, frivolous
favorite "You Made Me What I Am Today."

The pianist was one of my customers and I just
could not resist going backstage afterwards and asking him why he had chosen this particular tune at
that particular moment.

"Why," he said, "I thought that was perfectly clear.
Wasn't it the king's fault that she killed herself?"

In *The Prisoner of Zenda,* one of the famous pictures of the period, the heroine could be seen in her
boudoir arranging her beautiful hair in front of a
mirror. A young officer, mad with love, approached
her door. The door was locked. He tried to force it.
He hurled himself against it. But the door wouldn't
move. The heroine just kept on combing her beautiful hair. At last, with one kick of his brilliantly shined
boots, the enraged lover knocked down the door. The
glass came crashing down. He walked through the
debris, approached the heroine and found himself

rewarded for all his trouble with a resounding slap in the face.

The pianist who had to play this scene had to discharge a series of complicated tasks, typical of the lot of a movie musician of 1912. First he was required to play lovely music with one hand (indicating the lovely heroine) while the other hand had to mix in some sinister chords to signify the sneaky approach of the villain. As the lover kicked in the door the pianist had to lift a bag with broken glass and drop it at the right moment. A few seconds later he had to take his hands off the piano and slap them in perfect co-ordination with the haymaker on the screen.

Somehow it seemed that whenever I went to the movies, keenly interested in the musical goings-on, something went wrong. On this particular day the pianist in the pit somehow got lost in musical fantasies. He was still playing gentle tunes of love while on the screen the door was already crashing down. Then he seemed to awake. The music stopped. I could see him take up the bag of glass and drop it in perfect synchronization with the slap of the heroine's hand in the startled officer's face!

Soon the effects of all this made themselves felt in my daily work. More and more people began to write in for suggestions. What type of music did I think would go with a scene where Revenue Agents were dumping whisky in the city sewer? What kind of music could be used to portray Charlie Chaplin in a bullfight? We had an answer for every question. A man wrote in from Chicago describing in detail a picture which showed a scientist who had invented a serum which, injected into anything he chose, would change that anything back to its original form. The high point of the film came when the scientist administered a shot into a string of frankfurters. Within seconds a congregation of the strangest animals began walking off the table: dogs with cat tails, birds with four legs, midget horses with duck's feet. What, asked the man, can I play on my piano to go with this picture? I sent him a copy of Saint-Saëns' *Carnival of the Animals*, C.O.D., and I am sure he had a lot of fun with it.

More and more musical mishaps began to turn drama and tragedy on the screen into farce and disaster. More and more pianists, organists, conductors, came to ask us for advice. Exhibitors and theater managers made frantic efforts to avoid incidents that were becoming a serious menace. Carl Fischer's was probably the most famous and certainly the most successful house in the field of orchestra music. It was obvious that the people came to us. I began to understand their problems. We gave advice, we helped some of them, and when they described to us a particular scene in a film, we usually would know of a piece that would fit any given mood.

All this had, of course, a very stimulating effect on the volume of business transacted by Carl Fischer's orchestra department and as the orders came in I had visions of an even more magnificent future.

One day after I had gone home from work I could

not fall asleep. The hundreds and thousands of titles, the mountains of music that we had stored and catalogued and explored, kept going through my mind. There was music, surely, to fit *any* given situation in *any* picture. If we could only think of a way to let all these orchestra leaders and pianists and organists know what we had! If we could use our knowledge and experience not when it was too late but much earlier before they ever had to sit down and play, we would be able to sell them music not by the ton but by the trainload!

The thought suddenly electrified me. It was not a problem of getting the music; we had the music, plenty of it, any conceivable kind, more than anybody could ever want. It was a problem of promotion, timing and organization. I pulled back the blanket, turned on the light and went over to the little table in the corner, took a sheet of paper and began writing feverishly.

Here is what I wrote:

Music Cue Sheet
for
The Magic Valley
selected and compiled by M. Winkler

Cue No.

1   Opening—play Minuet No. 2 in G by Beethoven for ninety seconds until title on screen "Follow me Dear."

2   Play—"Dramatic Andante" by Vely for two minutes and ten seconds. Note: Play soft during

scene where mother enters. Play Cue No. 2 until
scene "hero leaving room."

3 Play—"Love Theme" by Lorenz—for one minute
and twenty seconds. Note: Play soft and slow
during conversations until title on screen "There
they go."

4 Play—"Stampede" by Simon for fifty-five seconds.
Note: Play fast and decrease or increase speed of
gallop in accordance with action on the screen.

I kept on writing for hours. *The Magic Valley* was
just an imaginary picture with imaginary scenes, situations and moods, but the music was real music. It
was music I knew. The endless years of close contact
with it, of carrying it around, of sorting it out, of
hearing it, listing it, handling it, living with it, now
began to bear unexpected fruit. I went to bed exhausted, and when I woke up the next morning it
took me a little time to remember how these densely
covered sheets of paper had come into my room.

The next day I copied them cleanly and wrote a
letter to the New York office of the Universal Film
Company.

"If you would give me a chance to see your pictures
before they are released I could prepare such a cue
sheet for every one of them," I wrote. "You could
send them out before you release the prints of your
films. It would give the local theater time to prepare
adequate musical accompaniment. It will help everybody, the industry, the musicians and the public." It
would also, of course, help the orchestra department
of Carl Fischer's and there was still another party I

was hoping the scheme might be able to help—but I didn't mention him in my letter....

Two days later I found myself in the office of Mr. Paul Gulick, publicity director of Universal in the Mecca Building, 1600 Broadway. It was late in the day. I had not dared to leave my job at the store, not even for so exciting an appointment. Gulick had my letter and the cue sheet for *The Magic Valley* before him on his desk. He began asking questions. What was I doing? What made me think that I would be the man to fit music to pictures? It wasn't just an occasional picture, he explained, there might be ten, fifteen, twenty every week—I wouldn't have time to go home and think and consult catalogues or listen to a lot of tunes till I found the right one.

"Just give me a chance," I said. "Let me try. I'll show you."

"All right—come up tomorrow night. Be here at seven. We'll see."

Between seven o'clock and a half hour past midnight the next day I had been shown sixteen different subjects—slapstick comedies, newsreels, a trip through the Sahara, a Westerner. I had been provided with a little desk, a stop watch, a stack of paper, a little mountain of pencils. I looked and stopped my watch and wrote. As the pictures flashed by, the bins in the Fischer store appeared before my eyes—I not only *heard* the music that would fit perfectly to the camels slowly swaying through the sand, I *saw* the bin that stored Tschaikowsky's "Dance Arabe" and the title in print and the little card I had written out

for the piece, and while the camels still trotted across
the screen I wrote it down on the cue sheet without
a moment's hesitation.

Gulick sat there, watched me and never said a
word. When I had finished at last, everything was
going in circles before my exhausted eyes. Gulick
took my notes.

"We'll let you know," he said, yawning. "Good
night."

I came home later than ever before. Even Mother
had gone to sleep. My supper was waiting on the
table. But I couldn't touch it. I fell into bed strug-
gling with the monotonous trot of the camels and the
galloping hooves that had carried Harry Carey to
his doom.

The next day—it was 3:30 in the afternoon and I
will never forget the day and the hour—a messenger
boy strolled into the Fischer store. He came over to
the orchestra counter. He didn't have to ask for me.
Before he could say a word I took the letter he held
in his hand, signed a receipt with a trembling scrawl
and went back to the dark corner where Louis
Werner used to open his pay envelope. I tore open
the envelope. It contained a letter signed by a live
vice-president of Universal, engaging me for a four-
week period to preview "the films made by this
company in advance of actual release date and to
prepare music cue sheets for said films, regardless of
character or length, such cue sheets to contain only
musical compositions published and easily available
to our distributors and exhibitors. The films will be

shown to you every Tuesday night at Projection Room C in our offices at 1600 Broadway. Your remuneration for said services will be $30.00 per session. If this meets with your approval please sign the enclosed copy and return same for our files."

It met with my approval. I signed the enclosed copy. I handed same to the messenger who was still waiting, looking with rapture at Jascha Heifetz who had just come into the store. Then I signaled to Werner and went downstairs. I walked through the aisles and the bins that had been my life for all these years. When I came to the little table and the chair where I had once been sitting, counting 2763 copies of "Your Lovely Eyes Smile at Me" I sat down. I covered my face with both hands and cried.

During the weeks to come I saw more silly comedies, blood-curdling murders and tear-milking melodramas than any other human being has ever been condemned to see. But nobody ever enjoyed going to the movies more! No sooner had I finished my nocturnal toil than Universal rushed my feverishly scribbled notes to the printer and the next day thousands of copies went out to every theater manager, pianist, organist and orchestra director in every movie theater in America. The response was overwhelming. Everybody was delighted. It seemed as simple as Columbus's egg—why had nobody thought of it before? Soon Universal was swamped with requests for cue sheets for films which had been released prior to my appearance on the scene and Gulick asked me to come in on Thursday night as well to see his old pictures. For the two evening sessions, each week, he offered me a salary of forty dollars.

Every year in the early spring you can see in the newspapers the pictures of people who have won the Irish Sweepstakes. Between one hour and the next their lives have been transformed: a barber in Brooklyn, a truck driver in Hollis, L. I., a housewife in the Bronx, a cook in a Manhattan hotel—suddenly singled out, suddenly touched by the fairy's magic wand. Their dreary lives, lives that never seemed to get anywhere, are suddenly changed as dishwashing machines, trips to Bermuda, fur coats, a house in Freeport are within their bewildered grasp. Every time I see their confused faces on the front page of the *World Telegram and Sun* and read the silly little conversations they have with benevolently bored reporters, I know exactly how they feel. They feel the way I felt when I got my first forty dollar check from Universal.

I hadn't won the Sweepstakes, though. I had more than doubled my weekly income by my own imagination and inventive capacity. I had done something all my own. I had always been told that America was the land of opportunity. Now, for the first time, opportunity had knocked at my own door. I had heard it knock and opened the door for it to come in. I was filled with happiness and pride.

Still, I didn't trust my good fortune. It all seemed too good to be true. I decided to put myself on probation for a few weeks at least. I wouldn't say anything to Father for the time being.

At home the waves of despair and excitement that followed the scuttling of our grocery business had slowly subsided. Jack was sending his regular contribution from Port Jervis. Herman was now doing the work I used to do in Carl Fischer's basement. Father had gone back to his pre-grocery routine: he again collected the bulk of our pay checks and paid for the household expenses and the rent. But Papa had changed. He spoke in low tones. He had become very quiet. From time to time the old spirit still flickered in his eyes. Then he would talk about grandiose schemes, about another store, bigger and better than the old one, about a factory, even about a gigantic sawmill he would put into operation "soon," somewhere far in the West! But it all lacked conviction. Often he was silent for hours, looking from the window down on the busy street or just sitting in a corner, brooding. I was sorry for him, the proud grand master of the past.

Only a few weeks after he had ceased to be an oh-so-silent partner in Father's grocery store, Dave came home one day, without his conductor's cap and coat. He had given up his job. His girl Ann and her family were moving to Hartford. He had decided to go with them.

"When are you leaving, Dave?"

"Tomorrow."

I went with him to the station. People looked at us as we paced up and down the platform. We really looked grotesquely alike. "After all, we knew each other before we were born," we used to say when people marveled at our identical faces, mannerisms, tonal expressions, eating habits, gaits. There had been our birthdays, the same beloved routine year after year: whoever woke up first would yell at the other one, "Hey, you louse, what about wishing your brother good luck?" There had been the school days and the fights on the streets of Radautz, there had been the horrifying experience in the Krakow railroad station when only our grotesque similarity had saved us from arrest and disaster. There had also been other experiences when a little uneasiness would creep into our relations. It happened, for instance, as Clara was telling me the same story twice.

"But you told me that story yesterday, Clara."

"Yesterday? I didn't even see you yesterday."

"But we walked here, on this same street."

"That wasn't you, Max, that was Dave I was talking to yesterday."

But it hadn't been Dave. It had been me. But some other time it might be Dave, Dave she was talking to and going to the park and sitting on a bench with under a mild spring moon. I'll wring your neck, Dave. . . .

And now my brother was leaving. We had never been separated, not for a single day in all these years. We walked up and down the platform.

"What will you be doing in Hartford, Dave?" I asked.

"Don't know yet. Try to get a job in a factory. Ann's brother is working in a gas station. Maybe he can help me. I'll manage."

Cold words. My brother is leaving. What can I say to make him feel how much I love him?

Nothing. Dave is going to Hartford, to live there and to work there and to get married. We are growing up. Dave is going to have his own life. He is leaving us. He'll never come back.

"Will you send Papa some money?"

"I'll try. I don't know. I'll do my best."

Cold words. He is already slipping away. And now it's time. "All aboard."

"Good-by, Max."

"Good-by, Dave."

Good-by. . . .

It was much more difficult to withhold the news of my new wealth from Clara. I saw her every day. We had in the four years of our acquaintance achieved an understanding and a communion of thought that made it almost impossible to leave anything untold. We had learned even to read each other's thoughts. It seemed almost unbearable to restrain myself, bubbling over as I was with pent-up excitement, joy and pride. Yet I didn't speak. I had a very special reason why I didn't. I had made up my mind that when the time would come to tell Clara about my position at Universal I would also talk to her about another, a very personal, and a very important matter, one that concerned only her and me, and one that would make Mr. Paul Gulick and his forty dollars look very insignificant. But I wanted first to be sure that Paul Gulick and his forty dollars weren't a mirage. I had gone through a hard school. I wasn't from Missouri, certainly not, but nevertheless I had to be shown.

So I kept my peace. I secretly switched or canceled some of my violin lessons and while Papa, Mama and bride-to-be thought me scraping away at fifty cents an hour, teaching a brat in Brooklyn the C-major scale, I was sitting in the drab splendor of the Mecca Building making forty dollars a week and writing cue sheets which within a matter of days would make thousands of men from Baltimore to Sacramento play the "Ave Maria" and the Theme from *Fingal's Cave*. It was a situation of eerie omnipotence.

Soon, however, an event occurred that convinced me that what had happened to me was no accident and that my life had at last taken a definite turn. It was on a Wednesday morning. I had come home late the night before—Universal had assembled a batch of not less than nineteen "short subjects" for the Tuesday night session and I had worked till the early hours of the morning. Then a few hours of uneasy sleep. I was dead tired and late for work when I saw a letter under the door. I picked it up sleepily.

I opened it. It came from the clerk of the District Court of Brooklyn. He said that he had the pleasure of asking me to come to the Courthouse next Wednesday at ten in the morning to receive my final citizenship papers. I stepped out of the house and took a deep breath. The morning air was cool and strong. I was wide and happily awake.

When the big day arrived, I asked Clara to come

with me. We both took the morning off. We had put
on our best clothes. As we had done for the past
four years every day, we met at 7:30 in the morning.
There was plenty of time till ten. We walked through
the streets and the avenues of an early New York
morning.

And now I knew it was the time and the right day
to tell Clara what had happened to me. Suddenly I
had lost all my fears and all my doubts. I told her
about my two jobs and about the nights I was spending at Universal, and about the violin lessons I hadn't
taught in all these weeks, about the money that was
suddenly "pouring in" and that had been put away,
every dime and every penny of it, in a new account
I had opened at the Dry Dock Savings Bank.

"The new account is in the name of Max and Clara
Winkler," I said.

"Max, what are you saying . . . ?" She had stopped
walking.

"I have been waiting for this day, Clara. I didn't
want to talk to you before I was ready and sure we
could manage. Now I am sure. In an hour I will be
an American citizen. We have to get married, Clara.
It's time. I know it and you know it. What do you
say?"

"Did you talk to your parents?"

"No. But I will, tonight. What do you say?"

"What can I say, Max? It's getting late. We have
to be in court in an hour. This is your big day, Max."

"This is our big day, Clara."

An hour later I raised my hand and spoke the

words of the oath and the clerk handed me a document, the name Max Winkler printed in big, beautiful
letters. I was an American citizen. Clara and I went
to a little restaurant in Brooklyn. We sat at a table
and ate. We took our time. Then we got up and went
back uptown to work.

I came home early that night. And so, as it had not
been in a very long time—how long I could scarcely
remember—it was a family dinner. Herman was at
the table, and sister Rose. Father was presiding.
Mother had set a lovely table. She put the food on
and sat down with us.

How long since I had looked at her like this! She
looked tired and old. My heart went out to her. Oh,
yes, I was what people called a "good son." I brought
home my weekly check. I had kept my promise to
keep our family together. I had taken on an added
and very heavy burden since Dave had moved to
Hartford. Just as I had known when we said
good-by in the station the day he had left, he never
sent any money; it was now all up to me. Yes, I had
tried to be a good son. But what signs of love, of
real tenderness, of the trembling affection that filled
me as I saw her now, had I ever given to her? We all
had accepted her silent service. Did she know that
I thought her the kindest, the most wonderful person
ever to grace the face of God's earth?

As long as I could remember I had never known
her as a really well person. She was a very tall
woman, heavy, lately very stout. Her feet had always

troubled her. She was suffering from periodical fainting spells. But never did she complain, never withhold from any single member of her family her
untiring silent service. Breakfast was ready at dawn
and dinner was still served with a loving hand in the
dark hours of the winter night.

Now, as I looked at her, I saw how old she was,
heavy, tired, worn out. . . .

I opened the big manila envelope and took out my
citizen papers. I was the first member of the family
who had been accepted into the liberty of the United
States.

Father took the document and looked at it for a
long time. Then I saw him bend down, quickly, and
touch the piece of paper with his lips in an intense
gesture of silent reverence. I had not seen him un-
bend like this in a long time, not since the days of
my early childhood when I had seen him kiss the
Bible after he read to us on Friday night.

Then the document made the rounds. Everybody
read it, marveled at it, commented on it with envy
and pride. At last it came back to me. I put it carefully back in its protecting container and laid it
aside. It was a gay, a happy meal.

Later Rose was sent to sleep and Herman, little
brother Herman, went out on a date. I was alone
with my parents. Mother took the dishes off the table.
We sat down, silent, content, feeling suddenly very
close to each other. I began to speak.

I told them what had happened to me during the
last weeks. I told them how my life had changed

overnight, told them about the money I was making,
about my new confidence and my new determination.
I assured them again that I would never desert them,
that they both would remain a part of my life
forever.

And then I told them that Clara and I intended to
get married.

I talked for a long time.

There was no reply at first. Father seemed absorbed
in deep thought. Mother, as always, was waiting for
him to render his decision.

How I loved them as I watched them sitting there,
looking so much older than I had ever noticed before.
In the silence I remembered the day Mother had
mentioned Clara to me for the first time. I had come
home late that day. She was still up, waiting to keep
me company while I ate my midnight supper. She
didn't ask where I had been so late. Instead she said,
smilingly:

"Is she a nice girl?"

"How do you know of her"—I felt myself blushing
in surprise—"Mother?" I said, looking at her good
face.

"Father has told me."

Father had told her! He had never met Clara, had
refused to have her in the house, had never mentioned her by name—but he must have watched me
all the time and had spoken to Mother about her.
That was Father. I'll never learn to know him.

Soon after I had that nocturnal talk with Mother
I had brought her to the house. Mother talked to her

for an hour. Then Father had come up from the store. He tried his best to be nice. He didn't quite succeed. After a little while I had taken her home.

But she had come again. After Father's fatal excursion into the grocery business had wiped out all our hopes and dreams, Clara was among the true and the loyal. She never wavered in her determination to stick it through with us. She assured Father and Mother that we, she and I, would never seek happiness for ourselves unless a way could be found to assure happiness for all.

It was then that Father began to look at her with different eyes.

"Did Max ever tell you that I didn't want to see or even know you?" he said with a tender gesture of apology to the young girl.

"Yes, he told me, Mr. Winkler," Clara said.

"I am sorry I ever said it," was Father's only comment. For him, it was a tremendous admission.

And now I had told him that we wanted to get married. I didn't ask. I just told him what was going to be.

I watched him sit there in silence. Suddenly the old fear gripped my heart. What would he say— would he shout, as he had done before, assert again his right to rule my life, accuse me of being unfaithful, or running out on him and Mother? Would there be another command? I knew that this time I wouldn't be able to obey.

At last I saw him light a cigarette, smiling shyly at Mother and then turning towards me.

"Have you talked to Clara's parents?" he asked.

"No. I talked to Clara and now to you. We wanted to know your decision first."

"I have no decision to make," Father said. "I have made too many already. They were not successful. I will not take it upon myself to direct your affairs any longer. I am ready and willing, and so is Mama, to abide by *your* decision. You tell us your plan."

I was thunderstruck. I never expected such a reply from a man who had never before tolerated advice, let alone ever thinking of following anybody else's lead. I wasn't prepared to answer.

"I have no plan," I said. "All I can tell you is that you will never regret your confidence."

Then I left the room. I had to be alone. I wandered around in our neighborhood for a long time. I walked, looked, wondered and worried. I felt a new sense of responsibility. A great change had occurred: I had suddenly been elevated from a boy to a man. From now on I was to be the guiding spirit of our family.

I was determined not to fail them.

11.

Simpson Street the next morning was a sparkling garden of roses. The Interborough Subway, a silent dream boat, seemed to glide gently through the hanging gardens of Nineveh. Downtown I saw old Louis Werner fly through the Fischer store, a friendly angel on snow-white wings. . . .

I smiled at him. I smiled at the customers. I smiled at Bebel and I smiled at Goetz. When Mr. Walter Fischer walked through the store I whistled, softly. A man asked me for a copy of Chopin's "Funeral March." I offered him Johann Strauss' "Wine, Women and Song" instead.

All throughout the day I was obsessed by the feeling that I had lost something. Was it my bankbook, my watch, the forty dollar check from Universal, my fiddle? No, they were all at hand. But something, surely, was missing, something was wrong. Suddenly I knew what it was. I had forgotten all about my stomach troubles. For a full day I had felt no pain. Later, on my way from work, I walked over to the bench on Cooper Square where I had spoken to the old doctor. I had to find him and to thank him for what he had done to me. But he wasn't there. Had he ever been there? Well, thank you anyway, Doc.

I walked away, dancing merrily through the rosy

mist of what once had been Third Avenue. Clara was waiting in the park. I told her about my talk with Father the night before.

"It is wonderful, Max. I am very happy."

"Yes, it's wonderful. And it's real. We will have a wonderful life."

"I know. I believe you. There is just one thing that worries me, Max. Where?"

"Where?"

"Yes, where are we going to have that wonderful life? I mean, just plain, where are we going to live?"

The rosy mist lifted. The park wasn't paradise any more. It was the Seventh Street Park in Manhattan, New York. The couple that occupied the adjoining bench had no wings. The girl was fat and had a freckled face and the man had a derby on his head and his pants were greasy and torn.

"We can't live with my parents," I said, after a while. "There isn't even enough room for us now."

"I have six unmarried sisters," Clara said. "We sure can't live at my house."

"No, I guess we can't."

"What are we going to do, Max?"

"Don't worry," I said. "It's quite simple: we'll buy a house."

"Stop kidding, Max. We haven't the money to buy the door mat."

"I am not kidding. We are going to buy a house."

The thought had never occurred to me before. Only a few weeks earlier it would have been utterly unthinkable. Now, all of a sudden, nothing was unthinkable any more. I wanted to get married. I had to take care of my parents. I couldn't afford to pay rent for two apartments. So I had to have a house to take care of everybody. And I was going to have one.

"We have two hundred and sixty-five dollars in the bank," I said. "I am a stock clerk at Carl Fischer's and a music master of the Universal Film Company. Why shouldn't we have a house? There is a whole new section of houses going up in Brooklyn. There are hundreds we can pick from. We'll get a mortgage. I'll borrow money from Fischer's. I'll get an advance from Universal. We are going to have our house, Clara."

"It's nice for a bride to move into a dream house, Max," Clara sighed, "but I can't see the house. I just see the dream. . . ."

"No, it's no dream. You'll have your dream house. And it will have a garden and a porch and on Sunday we'll sit on the lawn and watch our children play."

"Stop, silly."

"Just wait and see. I'll go home now. I'll talk to Father."

The man on the neighboring bench had his wings back. His girl was slim and beautiful, her skin had the angelic fragrance of a cherub. Third Avenue was back in its scented mist. I didn't go home. I didn't talk to Father that night. I stayed right there in the park with Clara and didn't talk at all.

But the next day I decided to talk to Father. For the first time there was no apprehension in my heart

as the crucial hour approached. Things had become
different. Our relations had changed.

When I told him about my plan to buy a house he
thought it was a great idea!

"I never liked it here," said the man who only a
short time ago had ruthlessly uprooted and herded us
all up here to the Bronx, the green flag of hope defiantly floating from his moving van. "If we had a
house Mother wouldn't have to climb all these terrible stairs any more," he said. "We will all live together—you and Clara and Mother and I and Herman
and Rose and maybe Jack will come back and Dave.
When do we move?"

And before I could get in a word he called out to
the kitchen: "Fanny, Max is going to buy you a house!
We are all moving to Brooklyn."

His unrestrained enthusiasm began to worry me. I
knew him too well. What was he up to?

"Now, take it easy, Papa," I said, trying to put
the brakes on. "I am just playing with an idea. Let's
not be too hasty about this. How much money do you
think we'll need?"

"Oh, a couple of thousand dollars for a down payment. I don't know exactly. But it'll be nothing to
worry about. An *Amerikaner* with two jobs who is
getting married should worry about a few thousand
bucks."

Ah, that's it! Papa is paying me back!

"Come on, Father, let's be serious about this."

By now I began to sweat. This was taking a serious
turn.

Then I saw a twinkle in his eye.

"All right, Big Shot," he said, "what seems to be the trouble?"

"Money—just money," I sputtered out, "nothing else."

"How much money do you have, Mr. House-owner?"

"I have two hundred and sixty-five dollars in the bank. But I am sure I could borrow . . ."

"You will not borrow anything from anybody. You take your two hundred and sixty-five dollars and buy some furniture and some coal so we won't freeze in the winter and maybe a few curtains for your Mother and a nice comfortable chair for her to sit in."

"And who is going to pay for the house?" I cried.

"I'll pay for it," he said.

There was a stunned silence as Mother and I looked at him in complete submission. Herr Verwalter Bernhard Winkler was back from the lumber camps of Rumania, brilliantly reinstated in his traditional position of splendor and grandeur. He walked over to the old bureau ($6.75 at Fishbein's at Second Avenue), and took out three bankbooks. He handed them to me. I opened them and looked at the pages, gasping for air. The three accounts of Bernhard Winkler I, II and III added up to $587.

"Father," I said at last, "but you were broke."

"Well, I was sort of, but I managed to save a little when they closed the store, and then when I went out buying food for Mother there was a dollar left

here and a dollar left there, a little there and a little
here and—oh, stop bothering me. Here it is. Take it.
It's yours."

And then summing up his supreme moment of
triumph he sat down in his chair, leaned back, blew
a large cloud of smoke leisurely in the air and said:

"It's all right, boy. Don't worry, Papa buys you
a house."

We talked about our plans till midnight. Herman
was sent downstairs to get all the newspapers. There
were houses for sale all over town. A down payment
of five hundred dollars would make us the owner of
a "fine two-story brick house with garden and porch,
hot-air heating system, all modern facilities." For
hours there was mighty scribbling of pencils. With a
small addition to our present rent, we finally figured
out, we would be able to pay for the mortgage, heat,
water and tax.

On Sunday the family started out early in the
morning. On 8th Street Clara joined the expedition.
All day we roamed around Brooklyn. We walked
through fine two-story brick houses with garden and
porch. We walked through one, through two, through
half a dozen. As night descended we had learned a
lot about the real estate business. We had learned
even more about human nature. But we hadn't
bought a house.

Another Sunday, another expedition. Fine two-
story brick houses with garden and porch and hot-
air heating system and all modern facilities—why did

they all sound so alluring when we read about them in the *Staatszeitung* and look so dreary and small and dark and moist and poor when we saw them and touched their walls and strolled through their empty rooms? After two more Sundays and twenty-two more fine brick houses we just gave up. We bought a two-family house at 2434 Cornelia Street, Ridgewood, Brooklyn, for $5700. Father handed over five hundred dollars to the man who had built the house. He was such a nice man. He told us that he had built three hundred more of these fine two-story brick houses. The man took the five hundred dollars, and for the balance of the purchase price gave us two mortgages, a first mortgage for four thousand dollars and a second mortgage for twelve hundred dollars.

This arrangement somewhat puzzled me, but who was I to argue with a man who had three hundred houses? On the first mortgage the man wanted an interest of 6 per cent. That sounded all right. It was the maximum the law permitted him to charge but it was all right. On the second mortgage the man wanted also 6 per cent interest. All right. And then the man went on:

"This second one," he said, "is just a small mortgage after all. It shouldn't bother you. You can pay that back easily in, shall we say, three years. Pay me, shall we say, fifty dollars or more every three months, that should be easy, and so in three years you'll get rid of it and can stop paying and worrying about the interest. Won't that be nice? It is all right? It is? Good, sign here."

We signed here and now we had a house. We paid the man his 6 per cent on the first mortgage and the 6 per cent on the second mortgage. Three hundred and twelve dollars per year. And on the second mortgage we paid him the fifty dollars he had requested every three months. That was another two hundred dollars per year. He had said "fifty dollars or more" but nobody had paid any attention to that and even if we had paid attention there was never any money left. And then the three years were over and the nice man paid us a visit.

"Your second mortgage is up, gentlemen," the nice man said, politely.

"What mortgage—we are paying interest and we are paying fifty dollars every three months. Here are the receipts."

"Sure," the man said, "you paid me six hundred dollars in three years. But this is a three-year mortgage of twelve hundred dollars. You still owe me six hundred dollars on it. And that money is due, today. So let's not argue. Just give me my money. I haven't much time."

"We'll keep on paying you fifty dollars every quarter, that's all we can afford."

"That won't do," the man said. "I need my money. If you can't pay up your mortgage you'll have to sell the house."

"We don't want to sell the house. You said fifty dollars every three months. . . ."

"Let's not get excited," said the man. "Maybe we can work that out."

We worked it out. The nice man canceled the old second mortgage and gave us a new second mortgage for one thousand dollars. The interest was, of course, again 6 per cent. It was again a three-year mortgage, payable at the rate of fifty dollars "or more" every three months!

So, after we had paid him six hundred dollars on the twelve-hundred-dollar mortgage we owed him again one thousand dollars on that same second mortgage! When we left our house in Cornelia Street after seven years of occupancy we had paid the nice man fourteen hundred dollars on the principal of his second mortgage plus 6 per cent interest—and we still owed him eight hundred dollars! Those were the happy days. . . .

The house on Cornelia Street—if I wrote it with a capital H it would sound like the alluring title to a thrilling mystery story. And there were indeed many mysteries in the house. There was, for example, the Mystery of the Windows. The house had three bay windows in front and three flat windows in the rear. But it had no windows on the sides. So there was a little light in the front rooms and a little light in the rear but absolutely no light in the middle.

Then there was the Mystery of the Hot-Air Heating System. In the cellar were two furnaces, one for each floor, but the only hot air they were ever able to produce must have been used up in the builder's sales talk. The more coal you put into the furnaces the more smoke you had in the house. As the furnaces became hotter and hotter the house became colder and colder because you had to open the three windows in front and the three windows in the rear and all the doors in between to get the smoke out. The smoke didn't get out but the cold winter air came in. Only the coal stoves in the kitchen with the upright hot-water tanks next to them kept us from freezing.

There were many other mysteries in the house but there was nothing mysterious about its two side walls. They were so-called party walls—one wall serving two houses. Every morning each house could listen to the coffee grinder of two other houses and no mystery ever veiled the snore, the cough, the sigh or the belch of your neighbor.

In spite of all this we felt like little millionaires. We were the owners of a house with six rooms upstairs and five rooms downstairs. Mother who had become still less agile and much stouter lately did not have to climb any stairs any more. I was living with Father and Mother and Herman and Rose in the downstairs apartment. The upstairs apartment was to be Clara's and my home. But we had so completely exhausted our financial resources that, even for a period of only a few months, it seemed extravagant to leave the apartment empty till Clara and I would be moving in. We decided therefore to rent it out. This proved to be a decision of extreme imprudence.

In our search for a suitable tenant we approached the nice man who had sold us our house. He strongly recommended a carpenter with a wife and a young child whom he described as "the cutest and smartest

kid you have ever seen." A day later our tenants
moved in. They paid twenty-seven dollars rent a
month and were to move out within two and a half
months. This we figured would give us time to clean
and to furnish the apartment in time for our wedding.

In the days and weeks to come there was a lot of
hammering going on upstairs, and no wonder, we
thought: after all, the man was a carpenter by trade
and making with a hammer was what he was here
for. The walls shook, Mother's dishes danced constantly with a melodic clang and once in a while,
when a particularly heavy blow fell, we could hear
a picture fall from the wall of our neighbor to the left
or a mirror crash to its doom from the adjoining wall
to the right. This however wasn't our problem. The
man paid his rent, we had neither pictures nor mirrors
to worry about and a little noise could easily be
absorbed for twenty-seven dollars a month. The
tenants mostly kept to themselves and little was seen
of the kid, who almost never seemed to leave the
house. Nobody, however, thought anything of it, not
until it was too late.

As the appointed day of their departure arrived,
the carpenter came downstairs, paid the thirteen
dollars and fifty cents he owed us for the last period
of his occupancy and, within a few minutes, began
carrying down his belongings and putting them on
the sidewalk. I helped him to load everything on a
little cart. He put his kid on top of it and soon we
saw them, man, wife and child, a picture of happiness
and contentment, walk down Cornelia Street and

disappear, forever, in the immense vastness of Brooklyn. It was a Sunday morning. Clara had come down to the house to join us in the happy occasion. Only a week still separated us from our wedding day. We went upstairs to look at what was soon to be our first home. Hand in hand we walked up the stairs.

Then there was a little cry and the next thing I saw was Clara, standing pale and wide-eyed in the door, one finger pointing in terror at something I didn't see.

And then I saw it.

The floor and the window sills, the walls, the doors, the window frames, just about everything, every spot in every room seemed covered by a web of tiny spots. First I didn't know what they were. As I stepped nearer I saw what Clara had seen at once. I saw that there were nails, hundreds, thousands, maybe millions of little wire nails hammered into everything that was made of wood. This had been the hammering day and night. A madman, a lunatic had been our tenant. But then it struck me as odd that the walls were only touched to a certain height—two feet, maybe a little more. There the march of devastation ended abruptly.

"The kid!" I heard Clara gasp.

Yes, of course, it had been the kid, the cute, smart little kid. He was a carpenter's kid. He didn't enjoy outdoor games. He stayed right in here and played as a carpenter's kid would play, with hammer and nails. Then I remembered the furniture I had put on the carpenter's cart only fifteen minutes ago. I remembered the chairs, and the table and the bed. And I knew with absolute certainty and could have taken an oath on it in any court that there wasn't a single nail in any of the carpenter's furniture. The kid was a carpenter's kid all right, but he was a smart carpenter's kid. He practiced only on other people's window sills.

Here, however, his devastating work had been complete. We had a week to prepare our new home, to furnish it with loving care, to paint walls and put up curtains and dream of the happy days ahead. We didn't dream or paint or furnish anything with loving care. For a full week we went down on our knees and pulled nails. We pulled them out with knives and scissors and pliers and teeth and with our bare hands. We filled three large barrels with them. The last nail was pulled out on the very morning that was to be our wedding day. I have retained from these weary days and back-breaking nights a lifelong aversion to carpenters, nails and tenants.

On Saturday, November 24, 1912, without pomp, pageantry, fanfares and flowers, in the presence of our God, our parents, and the four walls of a room, Clara and I were united in the holy bonds of matrimony, in accordance with the laws of the State of New York and in the tradition of the religion of our forefathers. We received not a single contribution of material value from either friends or family. Whatever we possessed was of our own making. Clara wanted to get married in a white dress of silk and a veil. She made them both herself.

I felt heartsick at the thought that the girl I loved more than anything in the world could not have a beautiful wedding dress, a lovely ring, a wedding with music and toasts and a gay crowd in attendance. But Clara had brushed aside all my misgivings.

"I have known you for more than five years," she said when I tormented myself with these thoughts. "We never were introduced to each other. We just started talking to each other one day, five years ago—and never stopped. We were never engaged, you never bought me any gift, you even forgot my birthday several times. Did I ever complain?"

I took her hand, silently.

"Three of my girl friends became engaged recently," she continued. "They were presented with expensive rings. They had big engagement parties. Two of them have already broken their engagements and returned their beautiful rings. Another one got married—with hundreds of relatives and friends witnessing the ceremony. I met her the other day. She doesn't look happy. Max, I don't need a ring and a party. I know that we are doing the right thing. We belong to each other. Our wedding will mean what God intended it to mean: to love and to cherish each other until death do us part."

Could any man ask for more? I covered her hands with kisses. I couldn't hold back the tears of happiness that moistened my eyes.

"One day, soon maybe," I said, at last, "you'll have

your ring and all the dresses and beautiful things any woman can ask for. And when our Silver Wedding comes around we will have a real party and we will invite hundreds of friends and relatives to make up for what you are missing now."

There were just enough chairs in our nail-scarred apartment to seat our six wedding guests—our parents, Herman and Rose. Mother had prepared a wonderful dinner with all the trimmings. After we had cut our cake, Father got up and made a little speech, serious and formal as if he were addressing a gathering of thousands in the Grand Ballroom of the Waldorf Astoria Hotel, summing up the gratitude that filled everybody's heart.

It was almost midnight before our guests left us.

The next day was Sunday. Monday morning I was back at work.

The house on Cornelia Street was now a very different house. Its dreariness was forgotten. It wasn't dark and cold and poor any more. It was our home. Clara had given up her job—I had insisted that she must do so the day we got married. The house was Clara, Clara by day and by night. Everything I did radiated from her. Going was from her, coming to her, thinking of her, working for her. Every step, every act, every word, every thought, the very purpose of living was my wife. Every little word became a big word. Every little act became an important act. Every little caress a source of happiness. Why can't I turn back the clock to live once more through these happy days? I am old today, but my heart feels young again when I turn back the pages of my life and remember our first year in the house on Cornelia Street.

And then, in the spring of 1914, the house was witness to still another important change in our lives: the arrival of Ethel, our first child. Today this child is a mother herself. I am watching her own little girl grow up. I can't remember my grown-up daughter as the little baby any more, our first baby that made us so happy and brought so much excitement to the house. But I remember when I think back to little Ethel's early days another mystery of our house: the Mystery of the Dumb-waiter. The first and second floors of the house were connected by one of those old-fashioned contraptions which you had to pull up and down yourself. When loaded upstairs, however, our dumb-waiter usually didn't need any pulling. It came crashing down and unless you were quick—and you weren't always—it put a few of your best fingers out of commission.

If you wanted to notify the party upstairs or the party downstairs that something was coming up or coming down you rattled a cord in the dumb-waiter shaft until the other party was ready. But even without any loads the dumb-waiter served as a prehistoric house telephone. If you rattled long enough somebody would answer and try to find out what the rattling was all about.

From the moment Ethel greeted the world that cord never stopped. Day and night my mother kept rattling it until one of us hollered down "Yes, Mother?" and Mother hollered up "I hear the baby cry." We had known that the baby cried. But we had overlooked the fact that parents' nerves are made of sterner stuff than a loving grandmother's gentle soul. So we took the baby up and the baby stopped crying and Grandmother downstairs stopped worrying and rattling the dumb-waiter cord. That happened many times during the night and after that succession of events had gone on for some time our little blessing had become the most spoiled brat in Brooklyn. She knew that all she had to do was to cry to get Grandmother to rattle the cord and Daddy to answer the call and Mama to take her up and carry her around.

It wasn't good for my mother to get up every time she heard the slightest sound upstairs. She hadn't been feeling well. Her fainting spells occurred more often and seemed of longer duration. Determined to stop Ethel from waking up my mother downstairs, we began taking her up even before she cried, obsessed with the idea of beating mother to the dumb-waiter shaft. Soon the kid caught on. The moment she felt a mattress she started yelling.

After several months of education Ethel at last was sufficiently trained to sleep all day and to cry all night! How we ever survived those long nights of sitting for hours in a rocking chair—a brand new piece of furniture which I had won in a puzzle contest— I shall never know. There Clara and I were sitting, changing shifts from hour to hour, rocking gently and incessantly in an effort to put the baby to sleep.

After an hour or two of rocking Ethel was quiet. I got up slowly and gently, very gently lowered her into her crib. On the downward motion she opened her eyes and by the time she touched the mattress she was yowling and crying as if we had put her on a bed of nails. . . .

It was in the pleasant month of June when we realized that the time had come to buy Ethel a carriage. It was the first time an exceptional demand was made on our carefully regulated budget. The price of the carriage was "only" twenty-six dollars. But it could as well have been twenty-six millions. I had neither. I made sixty-five dollars a week, a lot of money in 1914; but not for one who had a house with two mortgages—and with the kind of mortgages we *Dummköpfe* had put our signature to —and two families to support. By the time we had paid for the weekly installments on our furniture (my $265 had proven quite insufficient to furnish our house notwithstanding the fact that all our furniture was genuine Second Avenue and everything else in the house genuine Woolworth) we had about seven dollars left to feed ourselves for an entire week. Only a little while ago my sudden rise in the world of finance had seemed miraculous. But long before Einstein had proclaimed it I had learned that all things are relative. Sixty-five dollars sounded like a lot of money a year ago. Now I saw myself again at the brink of financial disaster.

Nobody else contributed a single solitary penny to the maintenance of our two-family establishment and its inhabitants. Jack had left Port Jervis to marry a girl whose father had once worked in the Rumanian forest under Papa's management. He just kept himself and his little family alive. Nothing could be expected from him.

Dave too had gotten married and had settled down in Hartford. From his scanty letters one had the impression that he was quite happily resigned to the fact that Max would be taking care of everything and that no news from home was good news. He never forgot our common birthday however. Year after year he wired me his best wishes.

As for Herman, he still lived with us. He had a girl friend and his theory was that times had changed and that it cost a lot more to go out with a girl than "in the old days." These days of yore were my own young days, the days gone only three or four years. But now I was a settled man with a wife and a child and in Herman's opinion had lost all touch with the merry world of a young bachelor. When once in a while I raised a slight objection or demanded some contribution from him I was brushed aside. I was getting old. I had no say any more in the affairs of the younger generation.

12.

In spite of all our troubles Clara and I were very very happy. We had learned early in life to pick on the good and pleasant things and to accept them as payment for our reverses, our sleepless nights, and our constant financial worries. We had our little house, we had our baby, we had ourselves in our upstairs paradise. Downstairs, Father, Mother and brother Herman had settled down. After a few months in the new surroundings, Father began rapidly to recover from the depressing memories of the excursion to the Bronx. Sometimes I felt like suggesting to him that it wouldn't be a bad idea if he would look for a job—but I never quite got up the courage.

You just *couldn't* ask Father to become an ordinary employee.

In the house he had again appointed himself master and manager of his downstairs section. He again told Mother what to cook—although one could notice a slight change in his attitude, indicating that he had never quite become the same since the collapse of his grocery business. On the last word of each sentence, whether it was beans, peas or lung *hache* he was ordering, he would now inject the polite hint of a question mark by slightly raising his voice. He didn't command—he suggested! His suggestions, however, sounded exactly like the orders of the good old days with a crippled exclamation mark replacing the upright one at the end of the sentence. But order or suggestions, Papa—or Pop as he now was called in the rapid progress of our Americanization—Pop was back with the groceries. As of yore he went shopping again, and this time he really felt that no other mortal was as competent to shop as he. Did he not go into the grocery business because of the knowledge he attained shopping for Mama—and wasn't he now highly qualified to do the shopping because of his experience in the grocery business?

Mother for the first time since she had come to America seemed relaxed and happy: she was living in a house near the ground, near the good earth, and the house provided her with a great and deeply appreciated pleasure, a garden. The magnificent garden the ads and the prospectus had spoken about was really the most miserable plot of desecrated earth I had ever seen. It was an eighteen by twenty piece of land, surrounded by houses and walls on all four sides. The sun would touch it for only a few hours each day but the smoke and dust, the ashes and refuse, the suffocating exhausts of the city came down on it incessantly.

Yet to Mother it was a piece of land. Since she had come to America, straight from the mountains and gardens and meadows where she had lived all her life, she had been spending her days in the stone deserts of apartment houses and city streets. Now, at last, she had a piece of soil again and at once she began digging and planting and caring for every square inch. She planted the things she had planted and seen growing at home: parsley, beans, beets, radishes. Excitedly she watched the first seedlings break the ground. She went through her little garden, watering the pitiful rows of sickly sprouts, waiting for them to grow, loosening the earth around them and watering them in the early hours of the day. In a corner of the plot was a little peach tree. Other trees that grow in Brooklyn have since become famous—but to my mother the little peach tree was the most important tree in the world.

The days of the harvest, however, were sad days. Mother still dreamed of the garden where she had once been planting flowers, fruit and vegetables, the garden at the edge of the great forests where wild flowers looked over the fence and butterflies came to visit and bees and clouds and sunshine. This was Brooklyn. The earth was contaminated by gas pipes and sewer systems. Bugs and insects swarmed around Mother's little plants. Her radishes were big and black outside but hollow and riddled inside. The beans were curled and dry. The beets were white, poorly colored by a few red streaks. And mother's tree never grew *any* peaches.

It was a great tragedy. All her heart went into the effort to grow things. Here she was, a daughter of the land, with all the instinct to till the soil and to make it produce, hemmed in in that miserable plot that would never respond to her loving care. She kept it up for a few years. At last she gave in.

Mother's garden, dead and deserted, was soon swallowed up by grass, dust and weeds.

On a Sunday afternoon I heard Mother cry out as if something terrible had happened. We rushed downstairs. She was sitting on a little bench that overlooked her garden and crying bitterly.

In the wilderness of the garden we saw little Ethel and one or two of her playmates. They had dragged Mother's famous sack of buttons out here on the grass and when we arrived they had just taken the last handful out of the treasure chest and spread it among the weeds.

We asked Ethel why she had done it.

"We were planting," she said. "We were planting blouses and coats and dresses and soon we'll come back to see them grow. . . ."

Even Mother had to smile.

But then she went down on her knees and began collecting her buttons. She didn't tolerate any help. She never stopped until she had covered every square inch of her garden. She painfully got to her feet, took up her sack and went back into the house.

That night she suffered another fainting spell.

These spells had occurred recently with increasing frequency and while they had happened occasionally ever since I remembered her they had lately begun to worry us. Mother had gotten paler and paler. She seemed to be able to move only with difficulty and this time, after she had come to again, she couldn't get up from her bed.

We had not spoken to her about our growing fears.

But now as Clara and I were sitting by her bed I decided to talk.

"Mother," I said, timidly groping for words, "you don't feel well lately."

"Oh, it will be all right soon," was her answer.

"What will be all right?" I asked.

She looked at me with a listless smile but made no reply. And then Father, who had been sitting in a corner, silently staring at nothing, got up and came over to where we were sitting.

He looked suddenly very small, stooped, broken, very much changed. For the first time in my life I saw tears in the eyes of the proudest, most confident man I ever knew.

"Mama is very sick," he said softly.

My heart stood still.

"Did you call in a doctor?" I asked.

"No. I know she will need an operation and I know that we haven't the money. Oh, Max, what are we going to do?"

"We will do what has to be done," Clara said, simply and firmly. We all looked at her gratefully. I took her hand.

"Listen, Mother," Clara continued, "don't worry. We will get our old family doctor to examine you. If you'll need an operation we will get the finest surgeon in the world."

It all sounded so simple. Suddenly we all were filled with new confidence. Father smiled and Mother seemed to look a little better. A few simple words spoken at the right time had brought a surgeon, a hospital, nurses and drugs to the house and nobody thought of the money to pay for it!

Clara called the old doctor. He examined Mother and then called us all out in the hall. Mother was suffering from a bleeding tumor, he told us. There was only one thing to do: operate at once. He pulled me away from Father who was again crying in despair and fear and whispered in my ear: "Work fast. She is bleeding to death."

His frank matter-of-fact words shook me into a cold apprehension of what we were facing.

"Doctor," I said, trying to keep calm, "tell me what to do and it will be done." Clara was standing by my side. I felt her hand in mine in a firm assurance that whatever I was doing was right.

"Have you got a phone?" the doctor inquired.

"No, but there is one in the store on the corner."

Clara, the doctor and I walked over to the store. The doctor went to the phone booth. We watched him take up the receiver. We couldn't hear what he said but we could see that he talked fast and that he did very little listening.

"Now listen carefully," he said after he had joined us again. "I have made arrangements for a private room at the St. Mark's Hospital for Tuesday morning. You, Max, will go there tomorrow morning, register your mother and just mention my name. You have to pay for the room one week in advance."

"Who will be the surgeon?" I said.

"His name is Dr. Leonard. He is a very famous specialist."

"What will his fee be?"

"About one week after the operation you will pay him three hundred dollars," the doctor said.

"One week *after* the operation?"

"Dr. Leonard doesn't charge for any operations that end in tragedy," the doctor replied. "That is why you will pay him later. Of course you must also provide for nurses, medicines and the operating room."

"How much will that be?" I said.

"About two hundred and fifty dollars."

"And your own fee, Doctor?"

"Don't worry. I'll see you at the hospital Tuesday morning. The main thing is to get Mother well. You'll pay me when it's all over."

After the doctor had left we didn't go home right away. We both were deep in thought. I had just undertaken to pay for an operation that would cost close to seven hundred dollars and didn't even know from where to take the fifty-nine dollars and fifty cents I would have to pay for the hospital room the next morning.

"Max," Clara said softly, "what is going to happen to us?"

"I don't know, Clara," I said, taking her arm as we began walking through the streets that Sunday afternoon the way we had done so many times and in so different a mood in the tender years of the past. "All I know is that Mother will be operated on. And if I can't get the money by the time I have to pay everybody I will fall on my knees and will beg them to wait. They will have to believe me and they will believe me, Clara, because you know and I know that I will pay them if I have to work for it for the rest of my life. I'll take the consequences no matter what they may be. The tumor must come out. That is all I know and that is all I care about."

"It's all right, Max," Clara said, "it's quite all right. Let's go home and tell Mother."

We turned around and went back. I felt happy in Clara's unwavering confidence. I wasn't going to disappoint her. All my life I had found that every time I had six ropes around my neck it took seven ropes to choke me. Something always happened before the last rope wound itself around my neck, and as we turned the corner into Cornelia Street I suddenly spoke out of my thoughts:

"Something will happen that will enable us to pay all these bills."

Clara made no reply. She just smiled and pressed my arm slightly as we reached our house. We told Mother that on Tuesday she was going to the hospital for an operation. Father didn't ask any questions. A few times during the following days it seemed as if he was going to ask the one fateful question that was on all our minds. But he always checked himself. We all had embarked on a silent conspiracy and the best thing was not to talk or even think of what the future might have in store for us.

The next morning I called the office of Universal and asked for an advance of eighty dollars. The request was granted without questioning. I picked up the money, went to the hospital, registered Mother and made the down payment for her room. I retained some of what was left to pay for the taxi that would bring her to the hospital. The rest, fifteen dollars, I gave to Clara when I came home.

"Hold on to it," I said, "there will be nothing coming out of Universal for the next two weeks."

Three days later Dr. Leonard performed one of his miracle operations on Mother. The doctors, the nurses and even the patient were all smiles when we came to visit her the next morning. The operation had been a full success.

After I had gone back to work I realized for the first time the full impact of my situation. But had I not always believed in miracles? Had not a solitary penny from heaven once saved my life and changed its entire course? Surely what I had done again deserved a break and as the days wore on I did not expect U.S. marshals and detectives to walk through the door from which I could not take my eyes any more, but a friendly messenger who would suddenly take me out of this horrifying nightmare, a messenger who would hand me again, as he had done in the past, my magic penny from heaven!

At about 4:30 in the afternoon a smartly dressed gentleman of about fifty-five years came through the door. He walked over to one of the boys asking for directions and was escorted to the orchestra department where he engaged in conversation with Mr. Werner.

After a minute or two Werner motioned me over.

"This is Max Winkler," Werner said to the gentle-man. "He knows a lot about picture music. I am sure he can help you."

The visitor introduced himself. "I am a theater manager," he said. "I have just booked for my circuit a film based on the opera *Carmen*, starring Geraldine Farrar."

Then he told me why he had come here. The Carmen film was a lengthy picture and while it was based on the story of Bizet's opera, it did, of course, not run in the same continuity. "There are outdoor scenes in the picture," the visitor explained. "There are ballets and a bullfight, scenes that could not be produced on the stage of an opera house. But we have them in the picture and we want to use Bizet's original music as much as possible. I need somebody to fit the score to the picture."

"Won't you sit down?" I said. He sat down and I began talking as I had never talked before. I explained to him that I had been doing this kind of work for Universal for a long time. "I will have to see the picture and will have to time every scene," I said. "I will have to study the original libretto of the opera and then I will have to fit Bizet's music to the action of the film. We will have to rearrange the orchestra parts. It's a big job but I think it can be done."

The visitor listened attentively. "When can you see the picture?" he said. "I have to work fast. We'll have our opening in three weeks."

"I'll see the picture tonight," I said.

"That's fine. Meet me at 6:30 on the twenty-fourth floor of the Chandler Building. By the way, what will you charge for the job?"

My God! Here it was. What was I to say? A whirlwind of nurses, surgeons, interns, hospital cashiers blew through my confused head. I made no reply. My visitor ignored my confusion. He looked at me coolly and said:

"Do you know Hugo Riesenfeld?"

"I certainly do," I said, relieved by the prospect of a few seconds of grace. Riesenfeld was a top man in the picture industry. He was the conductor at the Rivoli Theater, the first man who had brought movie music up to the lavish and spectacular standards of that lavish and spectacular period.

"Hugo Riesenfeld," my visitor continued, "was ready to do the job for a thousand dollars but he can't start working for another month. So I can't use him."

For a second I had to hold on to the counter with both hands. I felt the blood shoot into my head. A thousand dollars! I had been debating within myself during the last few minutes whether a hundred would scare him away! Here was my miracle.

"Let me see the picture first," I heard myself say with a voice that didn't seem my own. "Let's talk price afterwards. I'll see you tonight."

He left and I went back to work. Then I went to the Chandler Building. I had no chance to notify Clara that I wasn't coming home for dinner. As I rode up the elevator I felt dizzy with happiness and my heart was filled with a strange feeling of security and confidence that I had never known so completely before.

The man was waiting for me. He took me to the projection room. I had my tools with me, my stop watch, my pencils and my pads and began to work with furious concentration. After three hours I had timed every scene of the picture. The lights went on again and we went over to the office.

"I think I can do the job," I said. "I'll prepare a finished score for you in time for your opening."

"That's fine," the man said. "And now, what are your terms?"

"I have no terms," I said. "It's up to you to make terms. Because you see, I need this job more than anything else in the world." He looked at me in amazement.

I told him exactly what had happened to me. I told him what we had gone through during the past week and what we were hoping and praying for and what it meant to me when he had walked through that door and had come over to the counter. I just told him the truth, and I also told him that I couldn't possibly wait three weeks to get paid and needed some money before I was even able to start.

He did not once interrupt me. He sat there quietly, and looked me straight in the eyes.

"Of course you don't have to believe my story," I said at last. "But I can give you the name of the doctor and of the hospital and you can call up and check. . . ."

"I don't want to check," he said after a little while.

"I want to believe you. I have never heard anything like it in my life. It sounds unbelievable—but I want to believe you. I'll pay you seven hundred and fifty dollars for the job if you promise to finish it within three weeks. I'll have the check for you the first thing in the morning."

That evening, on my way home to Ridgewood, a ride on the Brooklyn Elevated of about fifty minutes, I had time to ponder about the events of the past six days. I was now thoroughly convinced that there exists an invisible, all-seeing and all-knowing power, helping those who help, and eventually destroying those who even contemplate destruction. All through my life, I had felt the existence of this power, but never before had I been blessed with so rich and abundant a reward. This time I had been doubly rewarded. What a wonderful feeling to know and to feel that I gave life to the person who had given it to me! It seemed to me that the long ride home that evening lasted but a few minutes. I sat with my eyes closed, dreaming of my good fortune, and thanking God for rewarding me so richly.

Two weeks later Mother came home from the hospital, radiant, rested and happy. Again we settled down to the normal routine of life. After all the bills had been taken care of there was enough left from that seven hundred and fifty dollars to provide Father with a new suit and a pair of shoes. The balance of forty-two dollars I gave to my wife so she could go out for the first time since we had been married to do the kind of shopping women like.

"Spend it all" was the first command I ever directed at my wife.

A few days later I received a telegram from Detroit:

> CARMEN MUSIC AND PICTURE TREMENDOUS
> SUCCESS. SEE YOU SOON. GET READY FOR MORE
> JOBS.

I read it and took a long look at the sky.

13.

In the succeeding years the film industry began to expand at an unprecedented rate. Soon what I had started on the spur of a moment had become a general practice throughout the industry. Other men had gone into the business of preparing cue sheets, and as for myself Universal had long ceased to be my only customer. I was now working regularly for Goldwyn, Fox, Metro and other giants and for the first time in my life I was earning real money. At last I gave up all my violin students and even so, when Harold, our second child, was born the baby carriage was no longer a problem.

I spent most of the days away from the store reviewing films and preparing cue sheets: as they listed Fischer music almost exclusively and promoted unprecedented sales of Fischer music in thousands of theaters it seemed to be an arrangement that was to everybody's advantage.

As my responsibilities and my success grew I began to move freely around the place where I once had trembled at every timid step. Everybody at Fischer's was requested to punch the time clock and even such veterans of the service as Werner or Kretzschmar were no exception. But I, with the benevolent connivance of benevolent young Walter Fischer, had given up checking in and checking out. Nobody said anything as I came and went on my busy errands, happy and convinced that everything was just fine.

It was, till one day early in July, 1918. An office boy was waiting for me as I rushed in in the middle of the morning and told me that the boss, Mr. Carl Fischer, wanted to see me at once. I went upstairs, full of pep and quite unsuspecting. The old man was in a terrible mood.

"I have seen you leaving the store today in the middle of the morning," he said. "You didn't even punch the time clock. I checked. You didn't punch it this morning either. Why aren't you at your station? What's going on here?"

I was utterly confused. Didn't he know? Wasn't he aware of what I was doing? I started to explain but he didn't let me finish.

"I understand that you are making a lot of money on my time," he continued. "You are working for film companies and while you take our salary you take their money too. It won't do. It has to be one or the other."

For a moment I wanted to explain that the deal he was offering me wouldn't do either. He wanted me to turn in to the house of Fischer the $125.00 I was making from the film companies in exchange for the twenty-one-dollar salary he was paying me! But I decided that nothing would convince him. He wanted time-clock punchers and all of a sudden while I was standing before him, I realized that I was no time-clock puncher any more.

"You either work for the film companies or for us,"

the old man said. "You will make your decision within the next few days. That's all."

The interview was ended. I walked downstairs, confused, disappointed, but not discouraged. I was suddenly faced with the necessity to make a vital decision that would change again the whole course of my life. Was I ready for it? Ready to give up security, small as it was; to renounce the accustomed and beloved routine of life and surroundings? But what else was there to do? I couldn't turn back. Or could I? Should I?

The next day, when I came back to the store, I was a very unhappy man. I had not realized until now what these many years had meant. I had become part of this place more than I wanted to admit to myself, and the place and the people in it had become part of my life. Here I had started as a greenhorn, I had suffered, fought, finally succeeded. And now this. Wasn't there any way out? It all sounded so wrong, so utterly undeserved. But then I knew the old man. There was no point arguing with him. He had put down his ultimatum and I had to take it or leave it. I avoided him for the rest of the day. I stalled for time. He had said a few days. One, two, maybe three or four, that was all. Then I had to act.

The telephone rang on Werner's desk. He picked it up, spoke a few words and then called me over.

"Call for you," he said.

I picked up the phone.

"This is Mr. Louis Selznick's secretary," the voice on the telephone explained. "Mr. Selznick is very annoyed with you. You got us in a mess and you better get us out of it again."

I had done a whole series of cue sheets for Louis Selznick recently. To get in trouble with the film industry now that the ground was giving in under my feet right here, was the last thing I wanted to happen. I felt panicky.

"What seems to be the trouble?" I said sweetly.

"You better come over here as soon as possible," the man said. "I can't explain it to you over the telephone."

"I'll be over tonight."

"You better be."

I spent the rest of the afternoon depressed, nervous, insecure. What a few hours can do! I didn't dare to leave the store before closing hours although I felt that I had every right to do so. I was back where I had started eleven years ago. When I left at six o'clock on the dot I punched the time clock. Then I rushed uptown to Selznick's office.

The secretary showed me a letter they had received from a man by the name of Sol P. Levy who complained bitterly about the fact that a song he had specially written for one of Louis Selznick's pictures had not appeared on my cue sheet. The picture had originally been produced by Rex Beach who had paid the composer for the song. Its lyrics even appeared on the screen.

"Why didn't you mention the fellow's song?" the secretary asked me, rubbing his hands gleefully. "The guy's probably going to sue us for one hundred

thousand dollars or a million or something and we are
going to sue you right back."

"I never knew of the song," I said. "Let me see the
cue sheet."

He took out the cue sheet. The picture ended with
an Indian in a canoe paddling away in a fade-out,
singing a song. This, Sol Levy stated in his letter, was
to be his song. I had written on the cue sheet: "Use
any good Indian song."

"I'd better go and see this fellow myself," I said to
the secretary.

"He'll probably throw you out," the secretary replied. "But here is his address, see what you can do."

I went over to the Columbia Theater on Seventh
Avenue and 47th Street. On the sixth floor I found the
office of Sol Levy. It was a small room, furnished with
a high desk, a couple of chairs and one old upright
piano. A tall dark man of athletic appearance was sitting at the desk eating a sandwich and an apple.

"My name is Max Winkler," I said. "I understand
you have written a song for a Rex Beach picture and
Mr. Selznick . . ."

He interrupted me with a gentle gesture of his
hand and a smile on his face, that took me by surprise. I had expected violence, rudeness, reproach,
but not this. "Mr. Winkler," he said, "just tell me why
didn't you mention my song? I had hoped so much
that the film would wake it up. Why didn't you mention it?"

"I'm very sorry I didn't," I said, "but to tell you the
truth I never knew your song existed."

"But it's published," he said, pointing to a pile of music stacked up in a corner. "Look here." He took a copy from the pile, blew the dust off and handed it to me.

"Mr. Levy," I said, glancing through the music, "all I can say is that I am working in the biggest music store in town. I think there isn't a song published that I don't know of—but I never saw or heard of yours."

He took a cigarette, offered me one and leaned back in his chair.

"I believe you," he said. "I think I have nobody to blame but myself. I'm just not a business man."

I felt sorry for the man. "What can we now do about it?" I said.

"I don't know," he said. "It's probably too late to do anything about it. I just haven't any luck, that's all."

The man's sad resignation to failure in a world where everybody else was madly scrambling for success touched me.

"Isn't there anything I can do?" I asked.

"Maybe there is," he said. "Maybe you could help me in some other way. A little while ago I wrote a waltz. I have no title for it and no words but I would like to play the tune for you. Maybe you could interest the house of Fischer in it. Would you like to hear it?"

"Sure, go right ahead," I said, glad that the subject had been changed.

He opened the piano and began to play. The little waltz had a tune of striking beauty and originality. I asked him to play it again.

"It sounds rather naughty," I said, unthinkingly, trying to sum up the peculiar rhythm of the little piece.

He turned around and jumped up. He was changed, suddenly flushed and excited. "Naughty, naughty, yes, that's it. The 'Naughty Waltz,' that's the title, that's the perfect name for it!"

"It's a great title and it's a great tune." A voice behind us suddenly chimed in. A man had come in the office while we were both too deeply absorbed with the music and our own thoughts to notice his arrival. I didn't know how long he had been standing there.

"Hello, Stanley," Levy greeted the stranger.

"Play it again," said Stanley. Sol Levy played it again, the man called Stanley humming the tune, stamping his feet, swaying entranced with the rhythm.

"Let me write the words for your 'Naughty Waltz,'" Stanley said at last. "I can use a couple of dollars right now."

Levy looked at me. "What do you think about it?" he asked.

"I like it," I said. "I like it very much. But why don't you publish it yourself?"

"I'll tell you why," Sol Levy said, smiling again his sad and touching smile, "I haven't got the money. That's reason enough, isn't it? But what about you publishing it? You like it, don't you?"

"O.K.," I said. "I'll publish it."

And there it was. I had made my decision. I had even spoken before I had time to think. But now it had been said and I knew that I wouldn't go back on my word. I would publish Sol Levy's song and that meant that I would start out in business for myself. My days at Carl Fischer's, my weekly salary checks, the established routine of my life—it all had come to an end. From now on I would be on my own.

Clara, when I told her at night, again inspired me with her loyalty, her complete confidence in anything I did. We talked long that night. I was about to make a decision heavy with frightening possibilities. We had managed, since the days of Mother's operation, to put aside seven hundred dollars from the money that came in, from time to time, through extra jobs I had been doing for the movie companies. These seven hundred dollars, our only reserve, were to be the capital of my new business. We had nothing else to fall back on.

The next day, the last day I was to spend in the old surroundings on Cooper Square, was not an easy one. This had been my home for eleven years. Here I had learned the rudiments of my trade, and had learned them in bitter lessons. The people in the store and in the offices, friends and foes, had been part of my life, and only now, when the hour of farewell was about to strike, did I realize how much it all meant to me.

I didn't go up to see the old man to tell him of my decision to leave. I went, instead, to see Walter Fischer, his son. He had not only been my immediate superior these last years: he had been a real inspiration to me ever since he had taken me out of the dungeons by his forever unforgettable "Good morning." I felt friendship and deep gratitude towards him and knew that I owed him more than anybody else.

I stood in the door to his office, my arms pressing against the door posts.

"You see," I said, trying to explain, "I can't stretch here any more. If I want to stretch, I have to walk out." And I stepped forward, out of the door, stretching my arms.

Walter Fischer took it all with a friendly smile. He got up and offered me his hand. I shook it, for the first time in my life.

"If you should ever be in trouble, Winkler," he said, "you can always come back to me."

I thanked him and left. I had no such fears. I went downstairs to say good-by to my old friendly enemies of the basement brigade. One of them, this very day, had brought with him a pair of little horseshoes which he had cut and carved out of a cigar box. They were neatly sawed and prettily painted in gay colors. Everybody admired them and the artist decided to dispose of them through the sale of twenty raffle tickets.

I bought two of them. Each ticket won one of the horseshoes.

I put them in my pocket and as I left the store of Carl Fischer's an hour later for the very last time I kept my fingers close around them.

I knew that I was going to need all the luck in the world.

14.

The next morning, the eighteenth of July, 1918, I was on my way to Sol Levy's office in the Columbia Theater, 701 Seventh Avenue. For the first time in eleven years a different trip, a different hour, a different place. For the first time in eleven years no fixed routine, no boss, no mail, no customers, no revolving door, no stairs to the basement, no voices through the dumb-waiter. New streets, new crowds, new faces and in my heart a new feeling of independent responsibility. In his little office I found Sol Levy waiting to see his publisher.

His publisher, that was I.

Soon Edwin Stanley arrived and we spent the morning talking and planning what to do with the "Naughty Waltz." Stanley was to write the lyrics. He didn't want to wait for royalties: he wanted money now and offered to do the job on a weekly salary. There I was, in business for exactly three hours, and already I had a lyric writer on my weekly payroll. In fact, I had to pay him his first week's salary right there and then.

It took Stanley three weeks to do the job. In the meantime I incorporated my business under the name of Cinema Music and went with Sol Levy over some of his earlier compositions which he had printed himself. Filled with great expectations, he turned them all over to Cinema Music. At last Stanley delivered the lyrics to the "Naughty Waltz," received his final pay check and departed. And now I had to delve into the diversified activities of a music publisher, groping my way with enthusiasm, courage and ignorance into the great unknown. I went around to see engravers and printers. I hired a man to make an orchestration for the "Naughty Waltz." I engaged an artist to draw a beautiful title page. I paid the printer and I paid the engraver and I paid the artist and I paid the man who had made the orchestration and, lo and behold, after a few weeks a thousand copies of the "Naughty Waltz" were delivered to our house in Ridgewood where they were solemnly received and stored in the basement by Cinema Music's new stock clerk. He was no other than Herr Verwalter Bernhard Winkler himself.

Yes, Father had accepted a "position" with Cinema Music. To be frank about it, it wasn't a salaried job—Cinema Music wasn't quite ready to hire a stock clerk. Father, nevertheless, took up his duties with great dignity and an iron devotion to duty. A stock clerk in a music publishing house occupies a rather humble station. It is his job to put music away when it arrives from the printer, keep records so that order fillers know where to find it and see to it that it is replaced in time and good order. To Father this job became at once the leading executive position in Cinema Music.

No matter how many times I tried to explain to

him that lumber yards and grocery stores are different from the music business, no matter how I tried
to impress him with the superior knowledge I thought
I had gathered during my eleven years at Fischer's,
he wouldn't listen. He did everything his own way—
and within two weeks had managed to organize our
entire business so that he was the only man who knew
what it was all about. I had explained to him, patiently, that stock is to be recorded on a card system.
He put everything in a book. He put it down in pencil, a thin, pale, always dull pencil, refusing the use
of ink and pen with the firm statement that American
blotters were no good. This book—it still haunts me
in my dreams—was neither alphabetical nor numeri-
cal. It was just Bernhard Winkler. To increase its
mysteries he wrote the old European figures—the
sevens looked like nines, the ones like sevens. The
figures were indecipherable, and other entries, written in his own, very private English, were completely
obscure. Nobody but he knew where to find a piece
of music. Nobody but he knew how many copies
were on hand, if indeed there were any. Whoever
wanted information had to come to him. He didn't
draw a salary but he was back in the lead. When I
tried to argue with him or to assert my position he
shut me up with a simple question. "Did you ever
get more for nothing?" he asked and went back to
his book.

He installed his office upstairs in his bedroom because, as he stated frankly, he didn't feel like an executive in the cellar. There he sat at his little desk

with his infernal book and a couple of old never-
sharps—and from time to time called out to the
kitchen for Mother to bring him a glass of water. She
came in, silent and devoted, and put the glass on the
desk of the busy executive.

When he spoke to his friends about his new position he was careful to explain that he wasn't really
working for his son. The son owned the business,
sure, but he, Papa, owned the son. . . .

After the thousand copies of the "Naughty Waltz"
had been paid for, the seven hundred dollars, the
capital of Cinema Music, had been invested down to
the last dime. It was high time for the firm to stop
spending and to start making some money. Sol Levy,
too, seemed eager to see some results of my labors.
Cinema Music had an agreement with him to pay
him one cent for every copy of his music sold and 25
per cent of what the firm would receive from the sale
of phonograph records and pianola rolls. The only
trouble was that there weren't any phonograph records or pianola rolls and no sales of copies of the
music either. I didn't know any vaudeville artists
who would sing our song and thus promote it—and
even if I had known them I didn't have the money
to make it worth their expensive while. All I knew
was how to promote music through cue sheets. But
even with the best of intentions I couldn't put the
"Naughty Waltz" and the half dozen other compositions of Sol Levy that represented the entire

catalogue of Cinema Music on every cue sheet I was preparing.

Sol and I smoked a lot of cigarettes and ate a lot of apples in the little office in the Columbia Theater but we didn't sell any music. I still had my regular income as a music spotter for Universal Pictures and a few other cue sheet customers, but the lack of the Fischer pay check made itself felt already on the menus as well as on the drawn faces at home. Something had to be done, and soon.

It was Sol Levy who came up with what sounded like a sensible idea.

"We are not the only people in the business who are too small to live and just a little too stubborn to die. There are others facing exactly the same problem. I know quite a few of them. Why fight each other and not get anywhere? Let's find out whether we couldn't join forces and, maybe, get at least somewhere."

The next day Sol brought with him a man by the name of S. M. Berg. I had known him by name: he had been one of my earliest followers in the art of making cue sheets for the films. He had built up a catalogue of his own and had published several hundred pieces all specifically written for film use. He knew of me, of course, and the idea of combining our catalogues and of trying to exploit our publications by using them on the cue sheets we were both preparing for an ever-increasing number of film companies appealed to him just as much as it appealed to me. Our two firms were merged into a new corporation, Belwin, Inc. It was a combination of *BE* from Berg, *L* from Levy and *WIN* from Winkler. It seemed a name easy to remember and the fact that the word *WIN* had been taken from my own name seemed to me a particularly lucky and meaningful coincidence. Our trademark was a bell hanging inside of a horseshoe. Berg and I each took 49 per cent of the new corporation. Sol Levy was presented with 2 per cent of the shares, thus giving him the power to referee and to decide any dispute that might arise between the two big shots.

Soon we went places. Berg and I had, in the past, been the real stars in the cue sheet world and now that we had become united, we established a virtual monopoly. We supplied the musical cue sheets for such famous film companies as Universal, Triangle Films (controlling Douglas Fairbanks, Sr., then, of course, very much Jr.), Wm. S. Hart, Fox Films, Vitagraph and Goldwyn, featuring the great M stars: Mabel Normand, Mary Garden and May Marsh. Every scene, every situation, character, action, emotion, every nationality, emergency, wind storm, rain storm and brain storm, every dancer, vamp, cowboy, thief, and gigolo, eskimos and zulus, emperors and street walkers, colibris and elephants—all this plus every printed title that flickered in the faces of the five-cent to twenty-five-cent audience had to be expressed in music, and soon we realized that Belwin's catalogue of so-called Dramatic and Incidental Music was quite insufficient to furnish the simply colossal amounts of music needed by an ever-expanding industry.

We searched for composers who would supply what we needed and we found them. They were fine musicians, but they were specialists in just one phase of music, film music, and most of them are forgotten today. Who still knows the compositions of Walter Simon, Herman Froml, Gaston Borch, Chas. Herbert, Irene Berge, Leo Kempinski, Maurice Baron, Hugo Riesenfeld? Very few, if any, will still remember them—and yet, in those days, gone only a few decades, their music was heard by more people in this country than the music of all the great masters combined. *Sic transit gloria mundi....*

In those days of the silent film, nickelodeons and song slides, these men created the only connecting link between the screen and the audience. The film companies and particularly the large theaters which employed orchestras, sometimes ranging to a hundred and more men, were clamoring for more and more music. Their instructions to us were: "Once we play a piece of music we don't want it duplicated for at least three months." This, of course, made our task even more difficult. Our composers were writing film music by the mile and in order to augment their own unceasing efforts we began to import music from Europe, where a whole battery of writers were busy turning their talents towards picture music. A.W. Ketelbey, world-famous composer of *In a Persian Market,* was among them, Ricardo Drigo whose Serenade from *Les Millions d'Arlequin* is still being played throughout the world, Giuseppe Becce, Patou—and even some of the works by the great Sibelius seemed to fit our purpose. Our catalogue of *Agitatos*, Animal Cartoonix, Church Music, and such titles as Sinister, Chase, Sad, Happy, Gypsy, Mysterious, Furious and Majestic grew and grew. But no matter how hard we pushed our composers, they had only twenty-four hours a day to put music on paper and that just wasn't enough. By now we were not only working for the film companies in New York: we had arrangements with some seventy theaters all over the country to view the pictures they booked and to make special musical cue sheets for their orchestras. The cue sheets plus the actual music was to be in their possession a week before the picture went on. Our demands grew into staggering dimensions.

In desperation we turned to crime. We began to dismember the great masters. We began to murder ruthlessly the works of Beethoven, Mozart, Grieg, J. S. Bach, Verdi, Bizet, Tschaikowsky and Wagner— everything that wasn't protected from our pilfering by copyright.

The immortal chorales of J. S. Bach became an "Adagio Lamentoso" ("for sad scenes"). Extracts from great symphonies and operas were hacked down to emerge again as "Sinister Mysterioso" by Beethoven or "Weird Moderato" by Tschaikowsky. Wagner's and Mendelssohn's Wedding Marches were used to portray mock marriages, fights between husbands and wives, and divorce scenes: we just had them played out of tune—a treatment known in the profession as "souring up the aisle." If they were to be used for happy endings we jazzed them up mercilessly. Finales from famous overtures, with *William Tell* and *Orpheus* the favorites, became galops. Meyerbeer's "Coronation March" was slowed down to a majestic Pomposo to give proper background to the inhabitants of Sing Sing's deathhouse. The "Blue Danube" was watered down to a minuet by a cruel change in tempo. Delibes' "Pizzicato Polka" made an excellent accompaniment to a sneaky night scene by counting "one-two" between each pizzicato. Any piece using a trombone prominently would infallibly be dedicated to the home-coming of a drunk: no other instrument could hiccup with such virtuosity.

Today I look in shame and awe at the printed copies of these mutilated masterpieces and I hope that this belated confession will grant me forgiveness for what I have done. But in those days these pieces saved our lives—no composer could ever catch up with me, blue-penciling and re-creating with scissors and paste a section of Beethoven's *Pastoral Symphony*. Soon we produced these "works" at a breathtaking speed and the Belwin list of Dramatic and Incidental Music covered about any situation even the most extravagant film writer could think of.

Unfortunately, however, among all these lovely musical harmonies, there began to develop a discord that soon grew in painful intensity. It hadn't been too long after Belwin had been established that I began to realize that Sam Berg and Max Winkler weren't

made for each other. We disagreed first on minor
matters such as the pricing of music or the construc-
tion of a sentence in our catalogue. But soon much
more serious matters began to develop. Berg was, I
believe, of English descent. He affected an aristocratic accent, his letters were fluent and distinguished.
My English was still of the Carpathian variety, flat-
flavored, with a New York East Side accent—and my
letters were short, direct and more often than not
grammatical conundrums.

It didn't take long for him to let me feel his "superiority." He began to treat me with contempt and on
many occasions publicly condemned himself for
having entered into a partnership with a man who
hadn't learned yet to wipe his nose the American
way. I began to hate him. I had gone through all this
before, in the early days at Carl Fischer's. I wasn't
going through it again. Soon every word he said
made me break out in invectives. I resented the high-
hat way he treated the customers, I resented the
way he ridiculed and criticized my letters, I even
resented the way he pronounced my name. We seldom spoke to each other and when we spoke it was
because we had something to disagree about. The
situation of Belwin, Inc. more and more looked like
collapse from within. One could smell troubles, even
against the wind.

About a year after Belwin had been incorporated,
things had reached the boiling point. Only Sol Levy
and his 2 per cent were still standing between Berg

and myself to prevent bloodshed. One morning I couldn't take it any more.

"Either you get out of Belwin or I do!" I shouted. "We just can't work together. I'll take ten thousand dollars to quit and leave you with the business if you will agree to do the same."

Berg roared with laughter. "Why don't you make it a million?" he said.

"I am quite serious," I continued, calming down a little. "Let's have an understanding, you and me. Whoever comes first and offers the other ten thousand dollars will own Belwin. Let's give each other thirty days."

Minority stockholder Levy sat down at the typewriter and drafted a contract. Berg and I both agreed to sell our 49 per cent in Belwin for ten thousand dollars to the partner who would come up with the money within thirty days.

"And what will happen after the thirty days are over?" Berg said. "You know that neither of us will ever see ten thousand dollars."

"If nothing happens we just will have to continue suffering together," I said. "It's worth trying."

"Certainly," said Berg. "I'll try anything to get rid of you."

We signed the agreement, gave a copy to Sol for safe-keeping and called it a day.

That night I didn't sleep much. I talked to Clara, telling her what I was about to do. As always, she backed me up and soothed my troubled heart with quiet confidence.

The next morning I went to see Mr. Walter S. Fischer.

A strange home-coming it was as I walked again into the store on Cooper Square. The old faces, the old surroundings, the stale smell of the store—it was all still there and yet, it was strangely different. It wasn't part of my life any more. I had become a stranger.

After a few minutes I was sitting in Walter Fischer's office.

"What brings you here, Winkler?" he asked.

I looked him straight in the eye.

"When I left," I said, "you told me to come back here any time I was in trouble. Well, I am in trouble now. So I came back."

"You want your job back?" he asked.

"No, Mr. Fischer. I came here to ask you to lend me ten thousand dollars."

He leaned back in his chair, looked up at the ceiling and for a while neither of us spoke.

"What do you need the money for?" he asked finally.

I told him what had happened to me since I had left Fischer's. I showed him a copy of the agreement I had made with Berg. He listened carefully.

"I don't think that anybody has ever asked a competitor to set him up in business," he said with his friendly smile. "What guarantees do you have?"

"I haven't any," I said.

When I left an hour later I had my ten thousand dollars. I had sold to Mr. Walter Fischer 49 per cent of the Belwin shares, the stock owned by Sam Berg, for five thousand dollars, and he had given me a loan of an additional five thousand dollars on nothing but my word and his belief in human character. Mr. Fischer had never to regret what he did for me. In the years since, until his death in 1945, I paid him dividends amounting to at least fifteen times his investment, and when I was able to buy back those shares from his estate and to regain complete control in my business I paid an additional large amount to the house of Fischer. Never have I spent money more joyfully and with greater pride.

Ten days later Berg was out of my sight. I was my own boss. The only thing that still troubled me was the fact that the "Naughty Waltz," the little song that had started it all, had been such a sad and complete disappointment. Again and again Sol Levy and I went around and showed copies to band leaders and vaudeville actors, but they only laughed at us. It was an impossible tune, they said, and a silly lyric and nobody in his right mind would ever inflict it on an audience. Of the thousand copies I had printed we still had seven hundred in the cellar and so we decided one day, a short while after Sam Berg had vanished from the scene forever, to take these copies and send them out at random and free of charge to every organist and movie orchestra leader we could think of. If nobody would buy, at least they would not refuse a present—and stock clerk Bernhard Winkler was worried about space.

A month later, and I will never forget the morning

when it happened, a telegram was delivered at the offices of Belwin, Inc. It came from Staunton, Virginia, and read: RUSH FIVE HUNDRED COPIES NAUGHTY WALTZ. KRESGE STORES. I handed the message to Sol. We both couldn't help laughing. For more than a year we had tried to give away our song. People wouldn't even take it for free. And now suddenly something had happened in Staunton, Virginia, something big and mysterious, and very wonderful. We had an order for five hundred copies but we didn't have a single copy of the "Naughty Waltz" left!

We decided to take a chance. We printed a thousand copies. We filled the order, trembling all the time at the thought that it all was a terrible mistake and that Kresge's wanted five and not five hundred copies and that we would have to sue Western Union for damages or commit suicide or something. But no, it was all on the level, a second large order arrived a week later, and before the month was over Staunton, Virginia, had absorbed 1150 copies of the "Naughty Waltz"!

What had happened? We had to find out. One of the seven hundred men on our mailing list who had received the free copies which we had given away in a last gesture of desperation was a man by the name of Ernest Atha, music director of the Strand Theater in Staunton, Virginia. He was the one man among all the seven hundred who had liked the song, had made himself a set of colored slides and had played the song with his little orchestra while the words were projected on the screen.

Mr. Atha certainly made history.

By September what had started as a spark in Staunton, Virginia, had spread like wildfire all over the country. Vaudeville performers picked up the song, dance bands clamored for orchestrations and soon copies arrived from the printers in truckloads, only to be shipped out again to the waiting multitudes as fast as they had come in. Never before had I tasted the sweet fruit of success. It was a new, a wonderful sensation and the bitter years of the past seemed wiped out in one mighty sweep.

Sol and I added another room to our office in the Columbia Theater, hired a young boy to help us, and from morning till night we just sat there, picked out orders from a large basket, counted copies and wrote out bills. I will never forget the morning when a stranger opened our door, looked in, saw me in my shirt sleeves counting out copies and approached me with the announcement that he was a composer and had come to see Mr. Winkler, the publisher of the "Naughty Waltz," about a song he had written.

"I am Mr. Winkler," I said, keeping on counting.

The man looked at me in consternation. "But I don't understand—are you *the* Max Winkler—what are you doing here?"

"I am filling orders, mister," I said. And, putting my finger to my lip to wet it, I continued: "See, every time I do this I make myself a nickel."

The composer retired in horror and I never saw

him again, poor man. All his ideas about a music publisher must have been shattered forever. I went back to counting out copies; then the telephone rang.

It was a call from Chicago. On the other end of the line was a Mr. Forster, the publisher of the famous "Missouri Waltz" and other hit songs.

"Mr. Winkler," he said, "I have the organization and the reputation to make a second 'Missouri Waltz' out of your song. Why don't we make a deal? Let me handle it for you. I'll print it and promote it and I'll pay you a royalty for every copy we sell and your share in gramophone records and pianola rolls."

I knew that the man was right. It was ridiculous to handle so tremendous an operation from a cellar in Brooklyn and from two little rooms in Manhattan. And I didn't feel myself yet ready to expand. I didn't trust my good fortune. I had seen Lady Luck come and go before. This time I was going to play it safe.

I made the deal with Forster. I transferred all the rights in the "Naughty Waltz" to his firm in Chicago. During the first four months of the agreement the Forster Music Company sold and paid us for 67,000 copies and for many years to come their semiannual checks provided Belwin with a solid operational base.

Only poor Sol had no part in it. When I handed him his first royalty check he placed his hands on my shoulders.

"Max," he said, "I haven't seen so much money at one time in many years. I owe it all to you. I want to go home and celebrate."

He went home and celebrated with his family. The

next day he came to work with a heavy cold. Within a few days he was on his back with pneumonia. All the money of his first royalty check was spent in a vain effort to save his life. Sol died within two weeks. It was a tragic and pathetic end of a tragic and pathetic life, just at the very moment when success and wealth were at long last within his grasp.

The success of the "Naughty Waltz" had established Belwin as a successful name in the music publishing world. I did not, however, intend to continue my ventures into the strange and perilous fields of popular music, now, after the "Naughty Waltz" had been successfully disposed of. My field still was picture music. It was the field I knew best, the one field I felt myself completely at ease in. Already the compositions I had acquired during the past represented a formidable list. It grew steadily in importance and sales volume. The best and most prolific writers of film music were now anxious to have their compositions included in my catalogue, and out of these associations, again almost by accident, a new sweeping success came my way.

The Fox Film Company had engaged Erno Rapee, the famous musical director of the Roxy who later became even better known throughout America when he took over the musical directorship of Radio City Music Hall, to prepare a music score for one of their most important films, the war picture *What Price Glory*. I had received a contract for the publication and distribution of the musical score. Rapee as-

sembled a large amount of music and composed
many sections himself. Among these selections was a
little melody which the orchestra played every time
the star of the picture, a *petite* Chinese girl by the
name of Charmaine, appeared on the screen. We
called the tune "The Charmaine Theme."

Soon, during rehearsals, the orchestra, the stage
hands, the ushers began to hum the little melody. I
persuaded Rapee to make a setting for it that could
be published and urged him to find a good lyric
writer who would set words to it.

A week or so later a man, holding a music manu-
script, entered my office. He said that his name was
Lew Pollock and that he had been sent there by Erno
Rapee.

"Sit down," I said, "anybody coming from Erno
Rapee is welcome here. What can I do for you?"

"Here is your lousy song," Mr. Pollock said. "I
couldn't refuse Rapee's request to write lyrics for it.
I understand you wish to publish it. It's fine by me if
you want to lose your money. But don't you dare to
put my name on the song."

"It's all the same to me," I said. "What name would
you like to have on the printed copy?"

"Just say 'Words by Louis Leazer.' That's the name
I always use for any piece of junk that isn't good
enough for Lew Pollock."

He left the manuscript and departed. I didn't see
him for several weeks. But when Lew Pollock came
again to the office he was a very different man. After
What Price Glory had opened at the Roxy, "Char-

maine" had become an immediate hit and was well on its way to becoming what it eventually was, one of the biggest hits of the decade. Mr. Pollock had come to ask that his name be restored on future printings of "Charmaine"! I didn't rub it in. I smiled and obliged.

I still have in my possession about a hundred copies of "Charmaine" with Louis Leazer as the writer of the words printed in the left corner. I keep them carefully. They help me never to forget that even the greatest experts in the music business know very little and that success and failure come to us suddenly, out of the dark, and usually when we expect them least.

While all this went on I began paying my debt to Walter Fischer. The loan of five thousand dollars had been repaid, and the dividends on his shares in Belwin increased from year to year. At the same time our personal relations, now on so different a level, grew through mutual respect. I was anxious, always, to show him my gratitude for what he had done for me and soon an occasion presented itself which, I felt not without pride, gave me a fine chance to show him and the house of Fischer what little Belwin was willing and able to do for them.

I have mentioned before Ricardo Drigo and his Serenade from *Les Millions d'Arlequin* as one of the great hits of the period. It was known throughout the country as the "Drigo Serenade." Fischer's who had the only American edition of the piece had sold many thousands of it. The piece had, of course, been a constant feature on my cue sheets.

One day in 1925 my friend Maurice Baron came to see me. He had just received a letter signed by Ricardo Drigo from Milan, Italy. Baron, then chief arranger for the Capitol Theater, had shortly before published a new orchestral setting of the "Drigo Serenade." The letter commented in most flattering language on Baron's brilliant arrangement, thanked him for what he had done to "my humble tune" and went on to inquire whether Signor Baron wouldn't like to try his "master's hand" on some other of Mr. Drigo's works. Fifteen of them were enclosed with the letter. "They might not quite fit the taste and requirements of your great country," wrote the composer, "but I have utmost confidence in you, my illustrious colleague, to adapt them in 'the American way.'" He added that he would let the great Maestro Baron do with them as he pleased and would be satisfied for his part with a remuneration of fifty dollars for each one of his fifteen tunes. "Please take care of my humble offerings which, under your masterful hand, will soon bloom into lovely flowers which I pray will be a source of joy to the citizens of your great republic."

Humble offerings they were indeed. Baron, while greatly honored by the praise and confidence showered on him by the great Drigo—nobody at the Capitol Theater had ever called him illustrious colleague and great maestro—frankly expressed amazement at the poor musical quality of Mr. Drigo's manuscripts. He had done the best he could to transform them into the lovely flowers that would bring joy to the citizens of our great republic and asked me whether I would like to publish them.

I had to decline with deep and sincere regret: Belwin just wasn't ready to absorb fifteen compositions by a single composer, even if he was the famous Ricardo Drigo. Here was my chance to show Walter Fischer that he had a real friend among his colleagues! I called him up, gave him the good news and Baron went right over to see him. Before he left I had picked three of the new Drigo works for the Belwin catalogue. Walter Fischer took ten, and Baron who also was a publisher decided to print one himself. That took care of fourteen of them. No. 15 was beyond repair. It went back to Milan with a check for seven hundred dollars and a letter of gratitude and appreciation from one illustrious maestro to another.

About a year later all fourteen Drigo works were on the market. Fischer's had done a spectacular job: they had published the ten compositions they had bought in a beautiful collection which they sold under the title "Drigo Collection: containing ten compositions by Ricardo Drigo, Composer of the world-famous ballet *Les Millions d'Arlequin*." It did well and so did the three Drigos which Belwin had brought out and the lonely horse that was running for Maurice Baron.

It was then that another letter arrived from Italy, addressed to the house of Carl Fischer. It protested in very outspoken words against the publication of "the most terrible music under my name. How dare you . . . I have never seen these miserable fabrications . . . a disgrace to my name . . . a blow to my reputation . . . a crime . . . an international outrage . . . I will take immediate steps in the courts of my country as well as in the United States. . . ."

The letter was signed by Ricardo Drigo. From the letterhead, from the style of the epistle, from the infuriated scrawl of the composer's signature—all so different from the gentle letter that had accompanied the humble offerings of the year before—there was no doubt that we had been made the victim of a brilliant impostor. It took the American Consulate in Milan only two weeks to ascertain the awful truth. No Ricardo Drigo was ever found at the address where our combined offering of seven hundred dollars had been received. The real Ricardo Drigo was terrible in his fury. The immediate withdrawal and destruction of the fourteen pseudo-Drigos was not enough to soothe his ire. He threatened all of us with damage suits that would have driven at least some of us into bankruptcy. Just when everything seemed to be messed up beyond repair poor Ricardo Drigo died. We were waiting for the heirs to take up the sword of vengeance—but nothing ever was heard from them. Up to this day they have remained silent. The storm had passed.

I have carefully refrained ever since from showing the house of Fischer my gratitude by offering them musical manuscripts.

I felt that my efforts might not be appreciated.

15.

Belwin began to develop into a prosperous concern. To the inhabitants of our two-family castle in Ridgewood this sudden prosperity was a new and quite overwhelming experience. It did strange things to us. Suddenly we didn't like our house any more. We wanted windows in our bedroom, we wanted free-standing walls, we began to resent the sound of the neighbor's sneeze. We discovered that our furniture was old and dilapidated. We felt that we needed a lot of things we had never needed before. What had seemed to be a dream house only a little while ago began to look like a dump. And so we sold the house on Cornelia Street and bought a new home in Borough Park, Brooklyn. It was a house with four free-standing walls and with windows. It even had a garage where, soon after we had moved in, a Dodge was ceremoniously installed.

Here, on June 6, 1921, we were blessed with Martin, our third child. Life at last was happily organized. There was, however, something that caused us a great deal of anxiety. Mother's health was failing. All my life I had been preaching and practicing the theory that if one has a thousand reasons to be unhappy and one reason to be happy to hang on with all the strength to that one reason for happiness. But now the situation had reversed itself. I had a thousand reasons to be happy and one reason to be unhappy and this one overshadowed everything else.

Mother was very ill. Her eyes were sad and misty. Every time I saw her I had the feeling that she was saying good-by. The inevitable finally happened.

On an evening in April, 1922, I was doing some work in our upstairs apartment. There was so much noise and commotion downstairs that I couldn't concentrate. I went down to find out what was going on. As I opened the door I saw Mother in an old-fashioned rocking chair joking and laughing with brother Herman. It was the first time in many months that I had seen her like that. She seemed so happy. I closed the door gently and left. I decided to do my work some other time.

It was the last time I saw her. She died in her sleep the same night.

It was the first time that death had come to our house. Every time I had seen a funeral it had been somebody else's. Every time we talked of death it had been a death in somebody else's house. And now it had happened to us. And at once the terrifying mechanics of death closed in on me. Death was not only the end of all things. People came to sell me what I had never thought of. Father insisted that I provide a place for him, next to Mother, so that "I can go home to her some day." I bought two graves and I had to rush to New York to make the bank five minutes before closing: the man who sold me the graves insisted on cash. "We can't take chances in our business," he said, with a terrifying sense of humor.

The last time I had seen Mother was in that rocking chair. I couldn't enter the room where she lay in state. I wanted to remember her, laughing loudly as she was seated in that rocking chair. Why hadn't I looked at her longer that last evening?

After the funeral I never entered the downstairs apartment again. Within four weeks we sold the house and moved to Lynbrook, Long Island. Father, Rose and Herman came with us. "When a mother dies," Clara had said, "the house breaks up forever." Father, who had been shaken beyond description by the loss, accepted gratefully.

Before we moved we sent what was left of Mother's belongings to a Home for the Aged. Among her treasures we also found that old sack of buttons. I hadn't seen it since the day when Ethel had spread its contents on the barren soil of Mother's garden. The sack had grown since. Mother had never stopped adding to her collection that now, after she was gone, brought back every day of her busy life. We decided to keep it. But when we reached Lynbrook it had disappeared. It must have slipped off the car and it was never recovered. To me, however, it remained present forever. Whenever I was confronted with a problem those buttons would whisper in my ear: "My child, this problem is only one button in the sack of thousands of buttons life has in store for you. Is it really so important? Just remember what happened to all my important buttons."

Yes, this sack of Mother's buttons that had seemed so important to her all her life and that had now disappeared into nowhere forever, served me well. Every time I was up against some problem I couldn't solve quickly, I just said "Buttons" and smiled and thought of something else. The next day that difficult problem wasn't important any more. It was just a little insignificant button, important yesterday, unimportant today and tomorrow—lost in transit.

Our new house in Lynbrook seemed to us an estate in miniature. It was a real country home, with a beautiful lawn, ever-blooming roses, lilac bushes, ramblers, a grape arbor and fruit trees. If only Mother could have seen it, she to whom even the miserable piece of ground in the back of a railroad flat in Brooklyn had meant so much. Many times Father would walk among those trees and flowers, crying softly. He had aged ten years in two months.

"It isn't easy to lose the grip of a hand you held for thirty-nine years," he told our neighbor. We all felt older, more mature, more aware of the problems of life.

Several months after I had seen him last at Mother's funeral, my brother Dave paid us a visit with his wife and two children. Dave, too, seemed a different man. For the first time since he had left our home after the grocery debacle he displayed interest in our affairs. In the past, the only connection he had maintained with us was the annual telephone call on the fifteenth of March, our birthday.

This time, before he went back to Hartford he asked us all to join him in the living room. He wanted to talk to us. He was pale and upset and spoke in grave and serious tones.

"I am now talking to all of you, Papa, Max and Clara," he said. "I have to ask a favor, a great favor from you. I haven't been much help in the past, I know. I now want to pay for the monument on Mother's grave. Please, Max, let me do it."

I had never lost that soft spot for Dave in my heart. Now all the bitterness and disappointment of the past was forgotten. I loved him more than ever before. I felt tears in my eyes as I embraced him. There was nothing I could say.

The monument was erected soon afterwards. Dave had come once more to be present on the day we all went out to the cemetery to dedicate it with a silent prayer. Father had written the inscription and we had followed his wishes to the last letter.

It read:

FANY WINKLER
You are still the wife of
BERNHARD WINKLER
and the mother of
David—Max—Jack—Herman—Rose

Next to it was a small, upright granite plate, covering the second grave I had bought at Father's insistence. Its inscription, too, had been written by father: RESERVED FOR B. WINKLER. SEE YOU SOON.

Dave's visits were the beginning of a renewed, intensified friendship. He and I were back to the intimate relation of our early days—and Ann, Dave's wife, and Clara seemed to like each other just as much. We began to pay them regular visits in Hartford. Dave was living with his family in a nice one-family house. He had a store in town where he sold automobile parts and accessories and was well known in many parts of Connecticut and nearby Massachusetts. Everybody knew Dave.

On my first visit to Hartford I found out how popular my twin brother was.

I had gotten lost in the maze of Hartford's one-way streets, trying in vain to find Park Street where Dave's store was located. I pulled up to the curb, stopped the car and blew my horn.

"Hey, mister," I called to a small group of men engaged in a street-corner conversation. "How do I get to Park Street?"

They looked at me and started laughing.

I asked them again. They thought it was all a great joke. I never got anybody to tell me how to get to Park Street. Most of them laughed—and some got rather mean about it. Twin brother Dave was too well known in the town.

As in the old school days, Dave and I enjoyed these mix-ups greatly. They had been part of our lives from our earliest childhood. They made us feel young again. Whenever one of us invaded the other one's home territory things were bound to happen.

I particularly like to think back to Dave's visit to

Lynbrook on the occasion of our fifteenth wedding anniversary. We had asked many of our neighbors to drop in for the occasion. Dave took his position on the front porch. Every one of our friends stopped to congratulate him before entering the house. Everybody was wishing Max a lot of luck by shaking Dave's hand. He stood on the porch, shaking hands, thanking and smiling for a full hour while I was talking to the guests inside telling everybody how nice it was to come here from Hartford and to be present at Max's anniversary. A conversation about last week's pinocle game finally caused Dave's downfall.

Yes, Dave and I were friends again. We shared our pleasures and our sorrows. And again and again our grotesque similarity played us hilarious tricks. The climax, however, came at one of Clara's and my visits to Hartford. We left Dave's house around midnight; it seemed a nice enough night for a stroll back to the hotel. But it was late and after a little while I hailed a passing cab and Clara and I got in.

"To the Bond Hotel," I told the driver.

When we arrived at the hotel Clara stepped through the door. I stayed to pay the driver. He motioned me to come closer.

"Don't worry, Dave," he whispered in my ear, "I ain't the kind of guy that squeals on a pal."

And he drove away, smiling and waving at me, frivolously pleased at the thought that Dave was going to the Bond Hotel with a lady that wasn't his own.

The years of 1927, 1928 and 1929 have gone down in history as the years of the boom and bust age. Those were the years of fifteen-dollar silk shirts, ten-dollar ties and fifty-cent cigars. Everybody who moved on two feet was a Wall Street expert. On every street corner you could hear excited discussions. I, too, was soon affected by the general rise in temperature and when the black Thursday in October 1929 arrived I, too, received a telephone call from a stockbroker.

"Rush down at least ten thousand dollars in cash!" he shouted.

"And if I don't?"

"Then your holdings will have to be sold at once," he shot back.

I just hung up. I had lost five thousand dollars, which I had originally invested, plus a wonderful amount of profits which I had made on paper. I wrote it all off as a good lesson. I had other things to worry about. The great crash that threatened every nook and corner of the American economic structure did not affect our business too much. It was a quite different event that brought, again, a threatening and complete crisis to my life.

Belwin had grown with the movie industry. From the days of the nickelodeon we had arrived at tremendous palaces that had sprung up all over the country. Music had become one of their big features. Hundred-thousand-dollar organs, sixty-piece orchestras, were advertised in screaming letters. Radio City Music Hall with a seating capacity of over seven thousand and an orchestra of a hundred and twenty-five was the ultimate and most colossal step in this nationwide development. The demand for music to go with the films was tremendous. It was an era of prosperity and a publisher who, as I did, specialized in music for the films and stayed away carefully from other adventures was bound to prosper with it. It seemed to be designed to last forever. And then, suddenly, it was all over, completely, with terrifying speed and with an absolute and crushing finality.

There had been rumors about an invention that could make pictures talk. We had shrugged them off. But then we all attended the grand opening of the first sound film, *The Jazz Singer*. That we couldn't shrug off any more. A few weeks later I had to realize that what had been an industry and what I had made my own and very special business, music for the silent films, would within a short time be a thing of the past. I went home, dazed, worried, concerned as I had not been in a long time. Again I was faced with the fact that there is no such thing as security. What I had thought to be a solid foundation of my life was again crumbling.

Within a few months fifteen thousand film theaters throughout the United States were clamoring for sound equipment. If one theater in a town was able to obtain it, every other house turned immediately into a morgue. Nearly one hundred thousand musicians found themselves without jobs. It was a grim, sweeping and disastrous collapse of a whole industry.

Belwin's tremendous stock of music had become

worthless over night. There was nothing to do but to face facts. I sold no less than seventy tons of printed music to a paper mill for fifteen cents a hundred pounds: $210 for the entire lot! It was the end of all my hopes and labors, and to top it with an ironic touch the paper mill that had bought my seventy tons of movie music after having been in business for over ninety years, went into bankruptcy two days before they were to pay me my $210. I never received a penny for my entire stock, the fruits of ten years of toil.

For a little while there was just nothing to do but to sit and wait and think of something that could replace my vanished empire. Was I destined to experience forever a mad succession of ups and downs? I did not despair. By now I had seen too many of these changes and I had acquired enough hope and confidence to take what was coming and to make the best of it.

Strangely enough the talkies which had dealt me so crushing a blow helped me again to catch my breath. The film companies began soon to realize that nobody could help them better with their new, uncharted task of fitting music to the sound track of pictures than the very men who had in the past done the same type of work for silent pictures. Soon fabulous prices were offered for the services of such men as Hugo Riesenfeld, conductor of the Rivoli Theater in New York, Erno Rapee of the Roxy or Nat Finston of the New York Rialto. Within a short time these men found themselves in Hollywood preparing musical

scores for the sound film, and what was more logical
for them than to fall back on the material which they
had used in the past and knew so well, their own
compositions as well as music by others, which was
published, catalogued, available—mood music Dramatic and Incidental that would fit to situations in
the sound film just as it had fitted to situations in
the silent pictures. The men who were selecting and
recording music in Hollywood were all my friends.
They knew every piece in the Belwin catalogue.
For the time being it was a life-saver to them and
for me. I didn't sell sheet music any more but I sold
to the film companies the right to use my music on
sound tracks. This soon became a general practice.
Belwin with its tremendous catalogue of dramatic
and incidental music was in business again.

But I knew that it couldn't last for long. The film
companies were paying millions of dollars to publishers and composers for the use of published music.
Soon they found it more profitable to hire composers
to write original music and to organize their own
publishing houses. When Warner Brothers spent a
million dollars to acquire the old established catalogue of M. Witmark and Sons with thousands of
valuable musical copyrights the rout was on. Soon
most of the major film companies were in the music
publishing business. They were not interested in outside publications any more. My catalogue, again, was
heading for the junk pile and this time for good. I
knew that if I wanted to survive I had to draw a

final line under the past and find an entirely new field of activity.

The end of what was left of my movie business was approaching rapidly and at the same time the ugly octopus of the depression threatened to squeeze the last bit of life out of the economic body of the country. I realized that I was facing a desperate situation. I was determined to remain in the music publishing field but I could not within a few weeks replace thousands of worthless *furiosos* and *mysteriosos* with new material. I had to create a new catalogue. It would take time, years maybe, and I didn't have time. And so the thought occurred to me that if I couldn't create what I needed to stay alive, I might be able to find what I wanted readymade somewhere else. America in the past had been of little interest to European publishers. But now with the rapid expansion of our own musical facilities this situation could well be reversed. If I could find a well-established European publisher who would entrust Belwin with their American representation, that would provide me with a new foundation on which again I could build and struggle and strive to succeed!

There was one particular catalogue I had set my heart on. In the golden days of cinema music, Belwin had become the sole selling agent for the catalogue of Hawkes & Son, London. They, like Belwin, had large amounts of "mood" music. Before he had given me his agency Ralph Hawkes had been represented in the U.S.A. by a well-established American house.

When he came to see me and offered me his agency I expressed my amazement. Why should he come to a newcomer, an outsider like me? His explanation was simple and quite frank. "With you," he said, "I am important. With them I am not. That's why I am coming to you."

He didn't have to regret his confidence. During the years of the picture boom I ordered his orchestrations of mood music in lots of a thousand and more for one single selection and even after the big crash I still sold some of his copyrights to the sound film. But now this all had fizzled out. Hawkes, however, had recently amalgamated his catalogue with another famous and well-established British house, the firm of Boosey & Co. The combination represented a powerful list of publications. It contained famous songs, such as "Bless This House," "Macushla," "Danny Boy," it had great Marches and other pieces for the band—a wealth of material that would provide an ideal catalogue if properly adapted.

I had nothing to offer these old, aristocratic houses in the form of prestige or financial evidence. My own catalogue was a dead thing of the past. Hawkes had known me only as a successful specialist in picture music—and that was little or no recommendation for so different and so important a field.

But I had to overcome the next few years. I had nothing to lose. It seemed worth while trying.

I decided to put on a big show, to travel to Europe in grand style and to impress the noble members of the British firm with the appearance of a confident, well-to-do and brilliant American music publisher. I put everything I had on this one card.

On June 30, 1933, Clara, the three children and I left for Europe.

16.

Two staterooms, waiters in
white jackets at noon and in red jackets at night,
a steward knocking at the door every afternoon to
ask whether he could lay out my evening clothes for
me, shuffleboard and a swimming pool for the children, tea and biscuits for the grownups, horse races
at night, an orchestra, a sun deck—this was my first
reunion with the sea since the days of the S.S. *Gerty!*
Never before had I so thoroughly realized what had
happened to my life, never before had I been so
grateful and so deeply touched by the blessings that
had been bestowed on me than when the five of us
were sliding down the bay, past the Statue of Liberty,
the skyline of New York not a strange miracle but
home, our home, slowly disappearing in the haze.

It was a lovely trip, gay, filled with the excitement
of a new experience and yet slightly overshadowed
by the anticipation of unknown decisions and un-
shaped events that were waiting for me. Their out-
come, I knew, was of fateful importance to me and
to our little family, and what began so gaily as a
pleasure trip, with all the offerings of luxury and
leisure gratefully accepted, might well end in disappointment and disaster. The days and the nights
passed rapidly, a trip that had taken me once almost
seven weeks took now just as many days and before

we knew it we were installed at the Mayfair Hotel in London. The next morning I passed Piccadilly and walked through the elegant bustle of Regent Street to present myself with all the confidence, self-assurance and courage I could muster at the dignified offices of Messrs. Boosey & Hawkes.

The reception I received, however, calmed my apprehension. Memories of the golden days when with every transatlantic mail Belwin's huge orders for film music had arrived seemed still alive in England. These inspiring memories of wealth and prosperity were of course closely associated with the man who had sent them and paid for them and so I soon discovered that I had an almost mythical reputation among these British gentlemen: the reputation of a commercial wizard whom they expected to do again for their catalogue in the educational and standard field in America what he had once done, under such different circumstances, in the field of picture music.

If I could sustain these impressions, I realized, something big was about to happen. When I came back the next day I was faced by the complete board of directors and two company lawyers. The seven of them sat on one side of the table and I, all by myself, on the other side. When they asked me whether I didn't require legal council I just looked at them and said, quietly: "I have full confidence in you, gentlemen."

A few days later my keenest anticipations had been surpassed. A new firm under the name of Boosey-Hawkes-Belwin was to be incorporated in

New York. It would be the sole selling agency for the United States for the combined catalogues of Boosey & Hawkes and of Belwin. It would be in complete control of all operations for this powerful combination of musical properties for the territories of the United States. I was to be the general manager and president of the new company.

The lawyers then retired and after two more days a lengthy document was produced. It stated every detail that was to govern the new organization and towards the end a whole page was devoted to define the duties of the general manager, what he was to do and what not. Eager as I was to consummate so tremendous a deal under any circumstances, I decided that I would never submit to these strangulating clauses.

"I am sure that you gentlemen know what you are doing," I said. "This is legal language. But it isn't my language. I told you that I was coming here without counselor because I trust you and I want you to trust me. This whole page has to come out of the agreement."

"And what should replace it?" one of the lawyers asked in a strained voice.

"I wrote it out on a piece of paper," I said. "It's very simple. Max Winkler shall be president and general manager of the corporation with full executive powers."

The meeting was adjourned. I went back to the hotel sure that I had gone too far and that it was all off.

When I came back the next day the contracts were ready for signature. The clause that I had proposed had been accepted! The biggest adventure of my life was to start under my own terms.

The agreement which I had made with Boosey & Hawkes remained in force for twelve years. Only in 1945, when both Boosey & Hawkes and Belwin had more ambitious and more independent ideas, did the association come to an end. By then, however, what had started out as a life saver for me had begun to become a burden. My own catalogue had grown to such tremendous proportions that I had no time left to worry about others.

A few more days were spent in London. The new General Manager and President of the American branch of Boosey & Hawkes was to meet everybody in the organization, was to get acquainted with their problems and their policy, was to see the factories, the printing plants, was to be introduced everywhere as was fitting to his elevated station. And then we said good-by to the seven gentlemen and to London and went on a real vacation, my first vacation in twenty-five years.

Paris, Switzerland, Vienna. To me all was loaded down with history and strange associations and it was all new, irreverently new to the three children who did not much care for all the sightseeing and for the delicacies of the French cuisine and were only happy after they discovered in the midst of Paris a restaurant named "The American Coffeeshop," operated by a former resident of Harlem, where they could eat pie à la mode and baked beans with ham. Vienna was filled with memories. When last I had passed through the city, it was the great emperor's mighty residence. How it had changed, wilted! To the children, though, it was still the town of music and laughter and we all went down to the Prater and to the castle of Schoenbrunn and to the chapel in the heart of the city where generations of emperors are buried. I was caught again, in spite of all the years, in the strange spell of history. Once I had been a subject of the emperor, his name had been carved in our young minds and hearts and as I walked among the sarcophagi I was touched by memories which I had thought gone forever. But it all meant nothing to the children, just a dark, damp cellar where they were not allowed to joke and to fight, and they pushed on and urged us to leave.

From Vienna the train took us still further east. Twenty-seven years suddenly were lifted, the mountains, the valleys, the trees and flowers, the houses, the boots and coats of the peasants, it all came back with overwhelming force and what had been buried deep, deep in my mind was there again, right there to see, to hear, to touch. The train slowed down and came to a stop. We got up and stepped down. I was back in Radautz.

The town had not changed. There was the schoolhouse, the store where I used to buy candy and fruit, the square where we had blackmailed Grandfather, the old house itself where Dave and I had lived, still inhabited by my aunts. But it all had undergone a strange change. It was still all the same, outwardly, but it had shrunk into ridiculous dimensions. It seemed a Lilliput town. The houses I had remembered were big and roomy. Now, as I entered them again, they were narrow, small and filthy. When I walked through the streets everything seemed within two city blocks. These had been long walks, filled with adventure, and now . . . even the old pear tree in the garden looked tiny, as if touched by a magic wand to fit in with the smallness of everything.

In my childhood days there flowed a little brook through the town. It was still there but it certainly smelled differently now.

We spent the first night in the old house where I was born and where my aunts still lived.

"Max," Aunt Malie said, "you are sleeping tonight in the bed you were born in." And then she told the children that they were to sleep in the beds their father and uncle David had slept in when they were little boys. Everybody was greatly impressed. The beds, the rooms, were full of memories and even the children, noisy, irreverent American brats as they were, became silent and thoughtful as they were sent to bed. But memories were not all that lived in these rooms. There survived also in those straw mattresses generations of fleas or whatever it was that caused an all-night epidemic of itching. The next morning we moved into a hotel. The beds were clean. We had candles, water pitchers, and basins in the room. The only thing we missed were field glasses to help us find the sanitary facilities which were way, way back behind the horse stables.

The arrival of the "Five Americans" had made a tremendous impression throughout Radautz. The town was buzzing. Relatives and old friends lined up to shake hands, exchange memories and, almost inevitably, ask for a little loan. Wherever we went we soon were the center of attraction and after I had tipped a waiter the equivalent of fifteen American cents, we were considered millionaires and everybody was bowing and walking backwards when we entered a shop or a restaurant.

A few days before we left, my uncle hired a big old bus with thirty seats and just as many rattling windows.

"Thursday at noon," he told the driver, "be in front of the hotel. We are all going to the railroad station to see Max and his family off."

Thursday at noon, thirty-two of us piled into that bus. Our baggage was stacked up in the aisles. One man had taken his seat next to the driver and was continuously pumping the big rubber ball of an old claxon horn as we wound our way through cows, geese, chickens, and a stunned crowd of citizens. At the railroad station we parked the bus and got out. Everybody, including the driver, sat down on the platform. At last the train arrived. We were rushed in, our bags carried by helpful hands, the door slammed and we were off.

As I looked out of the window, back to the old railroad station filled with waving, crying, shouting relatives and friends, I had to close my eyes for a moment. It seemed a dream. It was as if I could see my mother crying, waving good-by in the distance and Father smiling sadly, Father who had just smoked his first cigarette with his two boys as they were leaving, going away into the wide unknown world. . . .

But Mother was dead and Father was an old man in America. I turned around. The children were talking excitedly. They knew that we were going home. They were happy. They had already forgotten Radautz.

I took Clara's hand. She looked at me, smiling silently. She understood.

Two weeks later we were back in New York. There was no more time to think back. I had work to do.

17.

During the few months of our absence the country had changed perceptibly. One could smell the first signs of economic recovery in the air. Everybody and everything seemed to begin all over from scratch. The dark days of the depression were already fading into history. New hopes, new ideas swiftly took hold of the nation. It was in this optimistic atmosphere of new beginnings that I settled down to my new task. I began to organize the distribution of the wealth of material that my association with the British publisher had put at my disposal and, at the same time, looked around to see how Belwin, so sadly crushed out of a booming existence, could get back on its feet. Looking over the musical scene of America I felt that there were indeed possibilities which, properly explored and daringly exploited, could make even the most flamboyant days of the defunct movie business look pale and insignificant.

The United States had undergone sweeping musical changes. Within a few years thousands and thousands of bands and orchestras had been organized in schools all over the land. Full time music teachers had been added to the faculty of almost every high school. There wasn't a college, scarcely a public school in America, where a large group of students

would not participate actively in music. Some twenty-
five thousand bands and almost as many orchestras
were in operation—that meant millions of young
Americans playing an instrument. In addition there
were millions of youngsters using nothing but their
vocal chords. To a music publisher alert to the situation it could mean millions of new customers.

But how to go about it? I knew every musician in
movie land, but nobody in the new field of educational music. I knew nothing about the problems of
young students and their teachers. How does a school
go about forming and training a band? How teach a
boy of twelve to play the clarinet, the French horn,
the tuba? How does the teacher go about his business
when he visits the home of little Mary for the weekly
piano lesson?

The first group of works that I published will go
down in history as the most enthusiastic creations to
develop into the most devastating failures. My first
adventure was a series of books which I proudly
called Belwin Educational Library. Its No. 1 was an
Instinctive Method for the Violin, written by Arthur
Hartmann, a famous violinist and outstanding teacher.
His method was a masterpiece written by a master.
That was fine. What wasn't so fine was that the Instinctive Method was also written exclusively *for* a
master: within forty-eight pages it advanced the pupil
from a stumbling child into a brilliant virtuoso. It
might have been instinctive but it wasn't practical.
Both the author and his ambitious publisher had
overlooked the fact that there was one Arthur Hart-

mann to one million students who would have taken not 48 but 480 pages to master the Instinctive Method. I printed over a thousand copies of the book. Ten years after publication, in 1944, we took count: we still had 1022 of them on our shelves. The following year we committed 800 copies to the incinerator, keeping 210 in stock (12 copies must have died from starvation during the year)—only to find ourselves when we counted again a year later with a mysterious 487 copies. If ever a book had pups on the shelf, Educational Library No. 1 set the record.

This first adventure should have taught me that half knowledge is worse than no knowledge but it didn't. I followed it up with a series of books for children which I called Kindergarten Joys. They weren't. The words of the little songs were indeed beautiful. Listen:

> My doll can sing; my doll can dance
> My doll can talk and play
> You only need to hold her close
> And love her every day.

Charming words for a child of six. And charming music, I assure you. Only the music was within the ability of a child of, say, fifteen. So the babes who liked the words couldn't play the music and the teen-agers who could play the tunes refused to sing like a babe. That was the end of Educational Library No. 2.

No. 3 was a harmonica instructor, a fine and accomplished book indeed. I priced it, reasonably enough for all the wisdom it contained, at one dollar.

In those days a harmonica sold for twenty-five cents. Asking a dollar for an instruction book was like selling a piano for one hundred dollars and offering a piano method for four hundred. All this sounds like simple, logical facts. But you can't learn them from books. You have to learn them all through bitter experience. For instance: you publish—Educational Library No. 4—a Trombone Quartet. You rely on the name of the composer, a Heifetz of the Trombone. Who are you to question his musical station? Then after it has been printed the composer strokes the first copy gently and tells you: "Max, this quartet is so terrific I know only four trombone players who could really perform it—and one of them lives in Europe."

How I ever survived these years of apprenticeship I don't know. It soon became a question not of *what* to publish but of what *not* to publish. I realized that in order to participate in the education of young American music students I would have first to educate myself. In a newspaper article I came across some advice Thomas Edison offered to aspiring inventors: "If you want to invent something," he had said, "get acquainted with everything that has ever been written on the subject so that you may at least prevent yourself from traveling into alleys where others have failed." I couldn't get any advice from books. I had to get it from the people in the field. I had failed because I had made up my mind sitting at a desk in New York. I had never been in touch with life itself.

I decided to divorce myself from the confines of the four walls of my office. I decided to travel, and since then have covered every one of the forty-eight states, the District of Columbia, and every major town in Canada. Every spring I spend two hectic months preparing these trips. Every summer I am on the road. And I come back richer in knowledge, experience and ideas. I spend months turning what I have seen and heard into actual new publications.

The music dealers all over America have become not my customers but friends. I call the buyers, men or women, by their first names. I know the boss and his habits, I know the girls behind the music counter, I know the barbershop next door, the room clerk in the hotel, the streetcars, the busses and the movie theater in hundreds of American towns.

But once I had to discover it all for the first time and it makes me shiver when I think back to it. The planning and plotting of a trip in itself was a major and confusing problem. I looked at the map of the United States, drew a straight line between any two cities I wanted to visit and set out to the unknown wonders of the West.

Wherever I went I was a stranger. My catalogue was unimportant. Many dealers wouldn't even let me open my sample bag.

One of the very first stores I called on during my first trip taught me a lesson. I handed my card to the gentleman in charge. I opened my bag and began a carefully memorized lecture about the merits of my merchandise. The man listened for a short time. Then he took me gently by the arm, led me slowly to the door, opened it, tore up my card, said good-by and closed the door from the inside.

I was so stunned that I offered no resistance. I just walked away. When I came back the next year the man wouldn't even speak to me. I came back two years later and again the following year. I never made a sale.

The year after, when I opened the door to the store he looked at me.

"Hello," he said. "Are you here again?"

"I have to," I said. "It is my business. And I know that every time I come back I have a chance."

"Sit down," the man said.

He gave me a nice order. For the last fifteen years he has been one of my best friends.

It took me years to find out why I was a failure on the road. It took me a long time to realize that I was too enthusiastic, too anxious to sell, that I was like the man who goes to bed determined to sleep and as a result just cannot fall asleep. It took me a long time to lose the tormenting and humiliating complex that nobody likes a salesman. But after a little while I began to ask questions instead of making long speeches about myself and my merchandise. I began to get interested in my customers' business and in their problems. I began to learn from them instead of trying to teach them.

No matter how experienced you think you are, however, the trials and tribulations of a traveling man never end. Beaming happily he may stroll into a music store he has visited twenty-nine times in the past, only to be greeted with a cold "I never received your notice" or "Weren't you supposed to come the day after tomorrow? I'm busy today"—to quote only a few of the salutations that turn your happy expectations into resigned gloom.

But even if they expect you—and they once in a while do—there is an unending variety of characters that can make life miserable.

There is for example the buyer who goes out for a cup of coffee every two hours. Just when you think that he is ready to give you an order for five hundred copies of one of your songs, he'll say instead: "Let's go across the street for a bite." So you go across the street for a bite and he'll tell you all about Martha and the kids and by the time you go back to the store you know that there is only half an hour left and that you can't complete your order and have to stay overnight and that your whole schedule has been drowned in that cup of coffee.

Then there is the man who runs a music store and who knows all about pianos and radios and television sets but knows absolutely nothing about sheet music.

"Sorry, Max," he will say, "Alice does not feel well today. She does all the buying. How about seeing her tomorrow?"

Tomorrow of course you have an appointment in Albuquerque, an overnight trip from here. So as a last resort you phone Alice to inquire about her health, maybe she could come down before train time to talk just a little business. But Alice isn't even home. You say "Thank you," hang up the phone, forget all about Albuquerque and go to the movies.

The next morning Alice is in, and she is all cheers and how nice to see you, Max, and you begin working with her. But Alice isn't only a buyer. She is also a social lioness in the town and just as you begin going over the first page of your catalogue with her, your pencil poised eagerly on your order book, Mrs. Kemball comes into the store.

"Hello, dearie," Mrs. Kemball says and "Just a minute, Max," says Alice and goes over to Mrs. Kemball and you sit down wondering how many minutes a minute can last. After an hour and a half the minute is over and Alice comes back and you begin again where Mrs. Kemball threw you off. Ten minutes later Alice looks at the clock. "You'll have to excuse me, Max," she says. "I have to attend a wedding service. I am singing the Largo by Handel at Mrs. Fruntzenbacher's party." Alice has the finest soprano voice in town, damn it, and there she goes off to sing the Largo and you close your bag and your order book, all the time smiling at Alice till you are sure she is out of sight. Then you stop smiling for the rest of the day.

So much about Alice. Then there is Bernice. Bernice is the buyer you have to take out for lunch. She is no social lioness, she has no soprano voice and isn't invited to parties. So she takes it all out on you. She enjoys lunch. "Another cup of coffee?" "Sure,

another cup of coffee." Another cup, another cigarette—and all the time the clock keeps on ticking.
By 3:30 you get back to the store. You open your
sample bag and take out your order book. Just then a
customer comes in. That customer doesn't want to
talk to Jim or Jack or Jill. He wants to talk to Bernice.
So Bernice waits on him. It's a customer from out of
town. He has been waiting for this for three solid
months. He wants attention. Bernice is such a competent girl. The customer gets attention. At 5:30 the
store closes. You have no order. You miss your train.
But you can again go to the movies.

There is the ultrasystematic buyer and his twin,
the careless buyer. The ultrasystematic buyer goes
and checks and counts and touches every copy in the
store before buying a new one. He'll never get
through. It takes him two hours to check a single bin
and there are seventy in the store. You never have
a chance. "I'll send in the order," he says and there
is nothing you can do except grin and say "O.K.,
Jim" and leave the town. You write home to the
office that Jim will send in the order. He never does.

Jack, the careless buyer, is just the opposite. He
never looks at the stock. He reads through your lists
and catalogues the way he reads through a newspaper. "I'll take twenty copies of that and thirty-five
of this," he says. It's all mixed in with a lot of social
talk and peppered anecdotes. And after it is all over
you have a magnificent order. You wonder a little bit
how anybody can have such a marvelous memory
and just improvise everything he needs but who are

you to worry? You have your order and you send it home. A few months later you get a letter from Jack's boss. He received eleven cases full of music and he received that tremendous bill and what is going on here?—and you must have chloroformed Jack. Most of the music is returned and when you send him a credit you have to apologize on top of it.

But I still prefer Jack to Jill. Jill is the buyer who loves you and trusts you and will tell you: "Maxie, you go and check the stock yourself and make up your own order." My mother always used to say that when you go visiting and the hostess comes along with a tray of fine-looking fruit, don't help yourself. If you are smart you look at her smilingly and ask her to serve you, please. Because if you help yourself *you've* got to behave and if the hostess serves *she's* got to behave. The buyer who lets you make up your own order puts you strictly on the behaving side. It's good for her and it's very, very bad for you.

I know them all and I like them all. I have been a traveling man for a long time and I love every bit of it. Traveling has taught me to understand the tremendous, the unlimited possibilities of these United States. It has taught me to understand people. It has kept me open-minded, alert and young.

In these travels I learned one thing that I had overlooked when I had started out with my first clumsy attempts in educational publications. In public schools, high schools, colleges, academies, universities, music schools, summer camps and in millions of homes boys and girls were taking music lessons.

But as they progressed, from year to year, hundreds of thousands gave up. It was a large pyramid—huge at the base and getting thinner as it rose up. To my amazement I found that most of the composers I tried to work with were excellent architects. They knew how to construct a piece with a million and more notes on an acre or more of ground. What I needed was material for the masses that formed the base of the pyramid and in order to get it I had to find musical architects able to construct a piece of music with as few notes and on as little ground as possible: easy and melodious compositions, music that carried a message of knowledge, beauty and inspiration to the young student. I knew what I wanted and I decided to go out in the field and to find the men able and willing to give me what I thought to be right.

I organized my travels so as to be present at many of the conferences, clinics and conventions where music educators got together to discuss their problems, to listen to any number of bands, to try to organize this sudden, quite confusing and overwhelming onslaught of musical interest in every part of the United States. I joined the Music Educators Conference. I attended meetings of the National School Band Association. I began to learn, to observe, and slowly I felt myself walking on safer ground.

It was in those years that more and more band contests were put on, first in counties, then in states, then in still larger regions of the country and at last on a nationwide basis. Under the leadership of

A. R. McAllister, Executive President of the National School Orchestra Band Vocal Association, a series of national band contests was organized. The country was divided into ten regions, and by a slow elimination process bands were selected, rising slowly from contest to contest till at last, the winners of all ten regions found themselves pitted against each other.

One of my earliest adventures in the field was a contest of Region 3 in the city of Elkhart, Indiana. Bands had been classified as A, B, C and D bands depending on their proficiency. Twenty-seven A bands and more than fifty each of the B, C, and D class, each band with a membership of seventy-five players or more, had been pouring into Elkhart on specially chartered busses, trains, private cars and all kinds of vehicles including specially built trailers to carry the instruments. Every hotel and school, private homes and drugstores, lobbies and streets were bubbling over with gaily uniformed youngsters and from every street corner I could hear dozens of bands warming up. This was life, no theory. Ten years behind a desk in New York couldn't have taught me what I saw and heard.

The contest was to last for four days and there were sessions from morning till night. Many solo contests and lectures took place at the same time. Every school, every auditorium, the ballrooms of the hotels and every church and community center had been requisitioned.

Each band usually opened up with a march selected by its director so as to warm up the members and get them in a relaxed and happy mood. The march was not part of the contest performance. Afterwards, however, a work had to be played which the director had to select from a prescribed list of compositions, the so-called Contest List.

In the years to come the Contest Lists, published yearly throughout the United States, became for Belwin what the cue sheets of the old days had been for Belwin. Year after year I would prepare a large amount of music for the various classes of bands, for school orchestras, for every brass, wood, and percussion instrument, and for complicated combinations, submitting the music to various contest committees in the hope of getting them on the printed list, and soon I knew the right composer to furnish me with the material I needed.

At the conclusion of their performance and after they had played the "Required Number" (which the judges heard some fifty times played by fifty different bands within four days!) the band filed out. Their trials and tribulations, however, were not over. The big test for the musical standing of the band, for their alertness and general training, was still to come. It was the Sight Reading Test. Within ten or fifteen minutes after they had given their first performance they were led back to the hall—and knowing what was waiting for them most of them didn't look so good any more. Again they faced three solemn-looking judges. On each music stand the player found a large envelope containing the music of a composition nobody had ever seen before except the judges who had selected it. Even the director of the band did not know what he was to perform.

The chairman of the contest committee got up and spoke in a soft but commanding voice:

"Members of the band," he said, "will not touch the envelopes on the music stands until they are ordered to do so. The director will examine the conductor part at my given signal and will be allowed five minutes in which to acquaint himself with the score. When the five minutes are up I will signal you. You will then call your band to attention, each player will remove the music from its envelope and the band will start playing at once."

The conductor opened his envelope and began paging through the music. The band was silent. Tension was in the air. Suddenly the chairman commanded "Ready!"

Within a few seconds the music was out of the bags, the conductor rapped the band to attention and the performance started. They seemed to dive into the music with eagerness and enthusiasm. The conductor looked proud, the cheeks of the players were flushed, their eyes glistened. After the performance the players were ordered to place the music back into the envelopes so that everything would be in readiness for the next band that was already waiting outside.

Nothing, however, equals the excitement and the fun that prevails at a contest of Class D bands. The membership of these bands consists of boys and girls from ten to thirteen years of age, their repertoire is made up of easy compositions of short duration.

Practically every one of the players is accompanied
by a mother and a few other relatives, and a hall filled
with seventy-five mamas of seventy-five performers is
something not easily to be forgotten.

For two solid days I had listened to band music.
In the evening I talked band music and after midnight
I dreamt band music. But on the second night in Elkhart my dreams began to bother me. I awoke to the
strains of a clarinet going round and round in my
head. It was always the same melody, the same
cadenza, the same finale and the same wrong notes.
At last I realized I wasn't dreaming. It was an hour
past midnight. The sounds of the clarinet seemed to
come from somewhere across the hall. I got up to
shut the transom above my door but all I accomplished was to put a slight *sordino* on the music and
to change the sound from an annoying *forte* to a
tormenting *piano*. The last time I remembered looking at my watch by the light of the moon and the
sound of the clarinet it was 3 A.M.

The next morning I inquired where the solo contests for clarinet would take place. They were to
be given at two in the afternoon in the community
room of a nearby church. I went. I had to identify
last night's nightmare. Soloist after soloist appeared,
but none of them played my tune. I was ready to
leave when the last contestant was called up. There
was my nightmare! There was the melody, the
cadenza, the finale but, lo and behold, there were
no wrong notes. The boy won first place. I hadn't
suffered in vain.

This boy, a twelve-year-old bespectacled youngster from Billings, Montana, practicing a clarinet in a hotel room into the early hours of the morning, succeeding at last in overcoming every handicap and winning a difficult contest, has forever been to me a symbol and an inspiration.

Years have passed since and I have seen and heard many thousands of others who like him are taking part in the inspiring musical crusade that is changing rapidly the spiritual and cultural picture of the American scene. For many years it has been my good fortune to participate actively in these developments. It is from such youngsters, from their teachers and from their parents that I have learned and will never stop to learn. I listened, I learned and I acted. I had one great advantage—I was my own boss. The final power of deciding what to publish or what not to publish rested with me and with nobody else. Many of the salesmen traveling for some of my competitors were older and more experienced but they had to go back to their home offices, report their findings and observations to their superiors and by the time they were able to convince these men behind the desks that what they had found out in the field was the right thing to do, I was already on the other side of the mountain. Within a short time music educators were not only telling me what they wanted me to publish but they were searching with me and helping me to find the men and women who knew how to write the type of music that they themselves and their co-educators were looking for.

After ten years of consistent labor I felt that the Belwin catalogue had indeed reached a position in the field of educational music in this country that made me feel proud and secure. When, in 1945, I came to a parting of the ways with Boosey & Hawkes of London, this, too, seemed a logical progression of my life. No bitterness remained. I was ready to be alone, responsible only to myself.

Belwin had now established itself as an independent power in the field of educational music. Band and orchestra, every instrument, a large selection of chorus music had been established. I had been fighting for most of these works. Of a hundred manuscripts that I had received, ninety-nine were not accepted for publication the way they were submitted. Not that many of them weren't right musically—I just felt that they were wrong commercially. I insisted that they be adapted to what a student could understand. Hundreds of outstanding musicians all over the land have helped me in doing what I felt was right.

Yet, in spite of a success that filled me with pride and happiness, I was still not satisfied. There was missing in my catalogue the one prize I had been dreaming about ever since I had started out in business for myself. I craved a success in the field of piano music. I had tried many times. Educational Library No. 5 had been a work for piano—a collection of ten piano pieces in polyphonic style. They were by Boris Levinson, a prize pupil of the St. Petersburg Conservatory of Music and of such world-renowned masters as Glazunov and Rimsky-Korsakov. This, my first stab at the biggest field in music, had been a great success with the mice. They just ate it up.

Well, years had gone by since and I had become a little wiser. I knew that Levinson had been writing for the distant top of the pyramid. I knew that millions of pianos were installed in American homes. Millions of young people started out to learn. If I could address myself successfully to them . . .

I studied every new piece published by other houses. I asked my friends in every music store. There were more than 150,000 men and women teaching piano to more than three million students in thousands of private studios and homes. I was continually aware of a tremendous sales volume of piano music. To share in it became an obsession with me. Fate, or coincidence, or luck, or whatever you may call it, again put me on the right track.

I was on my way to Chicago one day, and on the train I met a salesman—an old friend who traveled for one of the large music publishing houses.

"Here is a funny one," he said. "There is a man by the name of John W. Schaum. He conducts a music school in Milwaukee. Recently he wrote an easy piano arrangement of 'The American Patrol' by Meacham and we published it. Imagine my predicament when I offered a dealer our Schaum arrangement and the dealer told me that he had just bought from a salesman for another house a hundred copies of the same piece arranged by the same Schaum.

The amazing part of it all was," concluded my friend, "that both arrangements were very easy, very excellent, and quite different."

I was electrified. There, I thought, is my man. Any man who can make two excellent, different and easy arrangements, of such a simple melody, must be a genius in his field. I decided at once to proceed to Milwaukee and see Mr. Schaum.

There I met a man, young, alert, practical, busy conducting a music school with hundreds of piano students. In fact he told me that he was much too busy to be bothered by a music publisher. I spoke to him at great length. I had a complete plan for a piano course to be augmented by many supplementary books and pieces. I told him what I wanted, without telling him how to do it. He gave in and went to work. Since these first memorable meetings in 1944, Schaum created, and I published, his piano course for young beginners (nine books), his piano course for adult beginners (seven books), and in addition more than fifty supplementary books and a hundred and seventy-five supplementary pieces, every one of them a best seller of staggering proportions. Collectively these books have become the most successful contemporary set of piano books and pieces within the memory of the music industry.

If I have in my deliberation revealed some of the secrets responsible for the success of Belwin, I have done so without fear of imitation. Several years ago, one of my more ambitious competitors engaged one of my best men. "Now," he said openly, "I will find out how Max is doing it." He soon found out that his formula didn't work, because the man he took away from me only knew what I had done, he couldn't know what I was going to do. I have always practiced the principle of studying my competitors carefully in order to be able to go back home and do everything differently.

Recently one of my competitors criticized me for promoting my publications through the distribution of free sample copies rather than through flowery language or doubtful endorsements. "How can you pay the rent after giving away so much music?" he asked.

My answer nearly floored him.

"I don't pay rent, brother," I said. "We just bought the building."

18.

Clara, in later years, accompanied me on many of my trips. Before we had realized it, Ethel was out of school, Harold was in college, Martin, our youngest, a senior in high school. Clara's constant presence at home was not required any more.

She loved and enjoyed the grandeur and beauty of our country, just as I did. It is a wonderful feeling to share beauty, even if it may be only the sight of a field flower, with someone you truly love. Our trips were journeys of never-to-be-forgotten pleasures and happiness.

These weeks and sometimes months spent together made us feel young and happy again. There were thousands of things to be discussed, or we enjoyed the even more precious hours of silence, riding together in a compartment, she clicking her needles, I scribbling on my notes. It was companionship of a great and affectionate communion.

"In about three months," I said to her on one of these trips, in the late summer of 1937, "in about three months we will have been together twenty-five years. Do you remember the promise I made you the day before we were married?"

"No," Clara said, "and anyway, you did a lot of talking twenty-five years ago."

"This was a very special promise," I said. "I had no flowers and no music and no present for you at our wedding and I felt quite badly about it."

"I remember that, Max—but it worked out all right, didn't it?"

"It did. But still—I promised you that when we celebrated our twenty-fifth anniversary I would make up for the flowers and the music and the friends that weren't at our wedding. That sounded like an awful long time then, like something that would never happen. But it's here now, Clara—in three months it will be our silver wedding. And you shall have it all—flowers, music, and friends, and even your slightly overdue engagement ring."

And she had it all, the way I had promised it when we moved into the nail-scarred upstairs paradise in Ridgewood. This time it was a brilliant gathering. We had hired rooms at a swanky catering place in Far Rockaway. Clara's mother, Mama Yetta, and my father were holding the places of honor. At the main table sat Clara, resplendent in the same silken dress she had made herself for her wedding twenty-five years ago! I, next to her, felt great in a tuxedo that was mine. Dave was there with his wife and family, brother Jack and sister Rose with her husband, and our children, Ethel, Harold and Martin. There were several hundred friends and neighbors.

Mama Yetta's entrance into the banquet hall, followed by my six sisters-in-law, had been a magnificent procession.

And as I looked over the sisters, their husbands and

children, I couldn't help feeling that I had made not too bad a choice among the seven. But they were all lovely people, a fine family, and good company at any time and particularly on a day like this.

Minnie was the oldest, the tallest and the darkest, the most ambitious among Mama Yetta's "Seven Dwarfs." She wasn't content to be a housewife. She was a successful designer and manufacturer of women's wear and had developed a very special vocabulary of her own. Nobody could call her children "kids": "Gangsters you call kids" was her pet admonition until she heard of the Quiz Kids of radio fame. Minnie, as myself, had many ups and downs. She was in and out of many business ventures, she enjoyed success and took her failures with the fortitude of a real trouper. As I write these lines Minnie is the manager of the custom-made department at Hattie Carnegie. I always thought kindly of Minnie. She bought the baby-carriage for our first-born. She was already married and out of the way when I approached Mama Yetta for the hand of Clara.

The only argument Mama had against our marriage was Sadie who was older than Clara. Somehow established standards and precedents made it a terrible crime plus a family and neighborhood scandal when a younger sister beat an older one to the altar. Sadie was of medium height, very much on the Emily Post side of behavior, insisting that her name was Sally, not Sadie. Every time we had a meal at her house I was meticulous in my behavior, sweating

it out in tie and coat, watching my table manners,
knowing that I was being watched all the time.

Then there was Gussie—more on the rotund side
of things—looking twice her actual size when standing near her very skinny husband Bert. You had to
know a lot if you wanted to keep up with her conversation. As if to emphasize her elevated station
in life she switched her name to Augusta and then
to Gusta. To the family she remained Gussie, though,
against her will and continuous protestations. Gussie
also played a pretty good piano, at least she thought
so. Gussie at her piano, myself with the fiddle and
Henry, Sadie's husband, with his collapsing baritone,
formed a Trio at the expense of our suffering neighbors. The "Holy City" was our favored piece. I am
afraid it sounded like Holy Hell.

Rose was known as "Strohsack," because of her
mop of tough, blond, curly hair. She was a violin
pupil of mine for a long time. Mama Yetta paid me
fifty cents a lesson. After several hundred of these
lessons she was about ready for a violin teacher. Rose
eventually made a Quartet out of our Trio, without
improving it in the least.

Norah, number five, was the darling and preferred
choice of Mama Yetta. She was the only widow
among the seven sisters. She never could do wrong
in the eyes of her mother—and all that love and understanding had been extended to Paul, Norah's husband. I always thought that Mama saw in him the
full-grown image of her own little boy whom she had

lost at the age of one week. Paul's death had been a terrible blow to both.

Number six was Regina, the tiniest, the wittiest and most effervescent little imp. She was and still is a terror. In later years she worked for me for a while as secretary. At the least provocation she would fly up in the air, until one day she threw a batch of letters, ready to be signed, right into my face, whereupon I fired her, creating a riot, hundreds of fainting spells in the family, and for the sake of peace, reengaged her. Fortunately she got married four weeks later, and quit the job.

It was a lovely, an unforgettable day. Father, already past seventy-eight, was presiding vigorously, drinking, smoking, assuming an air of utmost importance, deeply resenting the suggestions by slightly inspired guests that he and Mama Yetta should go, this very moment, and get married.

But there were also the empty chairs. There was an empty chair for Papa Max, Clara's father. There was an empty chair for my mother. There was an empty chair for my brother Herman who had died two years earlier—and one for Paul, the husband of Clara's sister Norah. I kept looking at the empty chairs. In the midst of the merrymaking they stood motionless, like tombstones in a gaily colored meadow. They brought back to my memory a picture I had seen as a boy many years ago in the home of a Rumanian peasant. It was a crude painting in loud colors. I still remembered every detail. The picture showed five steps leading up to a platform, and five steps leading down again. On the first step one could see a new-born infant. The second step on the way up was marked prominently with the figure ten. The infant had grown into a boy. The third step was marked with the figure twenty. The infant had now grown into a fine-looking young man. On the fourth step, marked thirty, you could see a fine young man. On the fifth step, forty, the same man looked somewhat older. On the platform he looked like fifty. Then the process downward began: sixty, seventy, eighty, ninety. On each step the man had grown older, grayer and more bent. On the fifth and final step was a small church, surrounded by a tiny cemetery.

Sitting at the festive table I closed my eyes and clearly saw that pyramid of life. I saw Clara and myself standing on the platform, looking back fifty years to the infant on the first step. We had come a long way, a long and arduous road, leading through dangerous curves and steep hills. We had gladly paid in tears, pain, and hard work for the great pleasures and happiness we had derived from walking up those steps together. We now stood on the top platform, fifty years of living and twenty-five years of a married and happy life behind us. We also looked down the other way towards that little church. Standing high on that platform, we could look both ways. We could see the infant as well as the church. We could see the baby on the first step up and its final resting place on the last step down. A prayer was in my heart that we might reach that last step on our way down, hand in hand, and walk into that little church together.

Within a few years the empty chairs around us multiplied. A film of Mama Yetta and her seven daughters, taken at our silver wedding, was to be the last picture of her. She died one year later at the age of seventy-one. With all of us she will be forever smiling and living in that film surrounded by her girls.

My brother Dave's visit to the silver wedding was to be his last visit to New York. Soon afterwards he became very ill.

During the years of his illness, we visited him frequently. Dave had retired from business and he had a lot of time on his hands. Our visits helped fill many of his empty days. In spite of the differences created by our two hearts, which were beating in two different tempi, we were still the twins of perfect identity. Our exterior features, our ways of expression and our mannerisms, even to the last detail of the wave of a hand in the course of conversation, were still the same. We were still the twin brothers of the days when Clara would insist that she had told me a story that she had told Dave the day before.

All of these identical characteristics were, however, in view only when we were both relaxed and seated. The moment one of us arose, they disappeared. Dave could walk only a few steps at a time. That was all his ailing heart would permit. The last time I saw him alive, he was standing in the middle of his living room, saying good-by to Clara, our children, and to me. I was the last to close the door on the way out. As I turned around to wave another good-by to him, he motioned me to come back.

"Max," he said, "my heart tells me that you will see me just once more, and that I will never see you again."

He spoke softly and slowly. I never realized until that moment how much effort it takes to move the human tongue.

"Max," he continued, "just stay with me a few more minutes."

He stretched his right hand towards me. I grasped it and covered it with my left. I couldn't talk.

"Max," Dave continued, "you and I were real brothers. We always considered ourselves big strong he-men. We always thought that babies kiss, men only shake hands. So you never kissed me—and—I never—kissed you. Let's do it now."

About two weeks later, at four in the morning, our phone rang. I jumped up. Since I had seen Dave the last time, I always jumped to the phone whenever it rang.

I knew what was coming.

"Who is talking?" I said.

"This is Charles, in Hartford. Is this you, Uncle Max?"

"Yes, Charles. What's the matter?"

"Our Pappy died, just a few minutes ago"—and Charles hung up.

The next morning we told Father, who was now eighty-four, that we were leaving for Hartford because Dave wasn't feeling well. I had never seen a dead person in my life, not even my mother. I remembered her only as she was sitting in that chair down-stairs the night she died, laughing and happy.

The evening before Dave's funeral, they all went to the chapel to be with him.

I stayed in the house where Dave had dwelled for so many years. I sat in his chair, my eyes closed, alone, thinking of my brother.

I saw him again standing in the living room, motioning me to come back and to kiss him good-by. I again heard his words, "Max, my heart tells me that you will see me just once more and that I will never see you again." I heard him repeat these words many times, in soft tones. Then it seemed as if he began to sing them. It was the tune of the "Funeral March" from Beethoven's *Eroica Symphony.* I had never heard him sing or whistle that melody before. "You will see me just once more, just once more, and I will never see you again." The day before his death, I had heard the New York Philharmonic Symphony perform the *Eroica Symphony.* The "Funeral March" had made me think of Dave, and now this saddest of sad melodies was ringing in my ears, in perfect synchronization with Dave's slow recitation: "You will see me just once more, and I will never see you again."

Suddenly I heard the door bell; Dave's wife, his family, and Clara were back from the chapel. I had been sitting in that chair for nearly two hours.

"Are you all right, Max?" Clara inquired.

"Oh, I am all right," I replied. "I want to see Dave."

"It's impossible now," Anne replied. "Tomorrow," she continued, "you will see him."

We were all there the next morning before noon, although the funeral services were not supposed to start before 2 P.M.

Dave was there too, or was it the other half of me that was there? Or was it me?

I just sat there in that chapel, motionless, tearless and painless. Dave looked in death as I looked in life! After the coffin had been closed, I found myself getting up and following the crowd like an automaton. Outside I saw people, staring and pointing at me. I heard one woman cry: "Look! You would think that Dave's ghost is standing there." To most people, it probably meant that his perfect image was just attending his twin brother's funeral. But to me, those searching eyes and pointing fingers made me feel that I was being buried. I was now paying for the gay time and for all of the happiness Dave and I had enjoyed, for the privilege of having been in the company of an identical twin for fifty-seven years.

On our way home to Lynbrook, I thought of a remark Dave had once made, when he was called upon to make an after-dinner speech. "Ladies and Gentlemen," he had said, "you over here," pointing at one of the men, "claim that you have known Max for thirty-two years. And you," pointing at another guest, "claim that you have known him for forty-one years." Then pointing at our father, he said: "And you, Mr. Winkler senior, claim that you have known him since birth. Well, I've got you all beat. I have known and lived with him long before he was born!"

I had lost a pal I had known and lived with, long before I was born....

When we arrived home, we found Father in the kitchen, sobbing. He had sensed what had happened.

"Max," he said, the moment we entered the kitchen. "Why didn't you let me go to Dave's funeral? It was Dave's funeral, wasn't it?"

It seems that old people are able to face tragedy with greater fortitude than people who have had less experience in the art of living. Father stopped crying. He rose in the slow motion so characteristic of old men. He looked at me, and in a falsetto voice said, "Max, it takes a lot of strength to cry and to suffer. I can't cry any more and I can't suffer any longer." He sat down again. "It is very painful and tragic," he continued, "for children to lose their parents. But this is the normal way of life. I will pray for the rest of my few days that God may spare you and Clara from seeing one of your own children taken away. God was good to Mama. He took her before he took Herman and Dave."

Father in his younger days was a tall, powerful man. Now past eighty-four, he was shorter in stature, his back was curved, his brilliant forehead smaller and somewhat caved in.

The loss of his second child was too much for Father. Several months later he died at the age of eighty-five, in his sleep, probably dreaming of his new home, where Mother dwelled.

When I visited him the last time—he was then living in a home for the aged in New York—he said to me: "You would think that a man who has been in the business of living for eighty-five years should know better than to lie down and die."

These strange words were the last I heard from him. Five hours later the doctor called me to tell me that he had died peacefully. Out there in the Washington Cemetery in Brooklyn, stand two tall stones made of granite. They touch each other. On one stone is inscribed: YOU ARE STILL THE WIFE OF BERNHARD WINKLER and on the other, the inscription reads: I AM STILL THE HUSBAND OF FANY WINKLER.

I was fifty-eight when Father died. When the old man was taken away from me, I not only lost my father, I lost also my childhood. No matter how old one may be, whether fifteen or fifty-eight, if one still has someone to call Father or Mother, one is still a child. With the death of my father, the last link to my childhood had gone. I had been moved up an entire generation. I was moved forward into life's front trenches.

My personal philosophy of living has always been predicated upon the theory—I had heard it expounded many times by my mother—that one should bless the thorns for producing beautiful roses, rather than curse the roses for having thorns.

I have no reason for changing my viewpoint. I feel

well rewarded for my labors, the pains, the trials and tribulations life has been handing me for the past sixty years. I shall probably continue to experience new sensations as long as I live. Some may be pleasures I have never experienced, others pains and disappointments. I will take them, the good things and the bad ones, as they come along.

I shall probably, in order to be happy, have to give up a little bit of my pride here and a little bit of my independence there. I may have to swallow a little bigger piece here and there. I may even have to choke a little bit in order to accomplish this, or I may be able to create an impression that I just did a little insignificant bit of coughing. I will probably eventually have to relinquish some authority and learn to share my earthly possessions with our children. I will of course have to make an effort to be a good father, and a good father-in-law, and a better grandfather.

Accomplishment of all these things should not be so difficult. All I have to do is to make up my mind to do it. Happiness, I found out long ago, is just a reflection of your mind. If I will therefore make up my mind that I am glad to live up to the duties and obligations imposed on a man past sixty, then I shall of course be happy.

The following is a clear example of what I mean. It was traditional with Dave to call me on the telephone on March fifteenth of every year and to exclaim, "Max! Congratulations—or is it my birthday?"

On the first March fifteenth after Dave's death,

Charles, his oldest boy, called me on the phone. "Hello, Uncle Max! Congratulations. I just want to continue some of the things my Pappy enjoyed so much." I never was much for tears, but there wasn't anything else I could do.

The second March fifteenth after Dave's death, and every March fifteenth thereafter, kept on passing into eternity without any congratulatory message from Charles. Should I, because Charles failed to maintain one of his father's traditions, work myself into a mental attitude of assuming that now that I am getting older nobody thinks of me and nobody likes me any more? Or should I say to myself, the kid is too busy and after all, he has to live his own life.

In all my expressions and resolutions about my philosophy and the art of living, I have, whenever I said "I" meant "we," and whenever I spoke of myself as "father," "father-in-law" and "grandfather," I also meant "mother," "mother-in-law" and "grandmother." For Clara has always fully shared my views, and I know that she will continue to remain my full-fledged partner in everything that life may have in store for us. The only thing that we may have to do separately is to die separately and providence may even prevent that.

I find life in the front trenches, at the age of sixty-one, not easy, and at times, extremely complicated.

During the days when Clara and I were just recruits, all we had to contend with were two characters, hers and mine. Now we have in addition to ourselves, not only the three characters we ourselves brought into the world, but also the three characters they married, plus four little characters called our grandchildren.

The possibilities therefore of someone getting a cold, or getting hurt, are greatly multiplied. There is also the problem of getting along with six grown-ups and four little characters. Whereas in the past, all we had to do was to get along with each other. Our motto was, and must therefore remain, *To get along*. If the wife of one of our sons should pass our house without knocking at our door, we should like to believe that she was probably too busy, rather than assume that she passed us up intentionally.

And while on the subject of the characters our children married, I must mention that Ethel is now married to Paul. We all love him. He is a man with a heart bigger than his six feet three. Paul is worthy of the honor of being called a good son, a good husband, and a father to little Joan.

We decided to use our long experience of living, not for the purpose of building an exit for ourselves, but rather to help our children build their own castles. Clara ofttimes feels that we are doing too much for our children. Whenever this subject comes up, I remind her of an experience my father had in Florida, where I used to send him to spend the late winters of his life. Father met a Mr. Henley there. He was seventy-nine years old. This Mr. Henley had just bought himself a yacht for which he had paid $60,000.

"At your age you spend $60,000 for a boat?" Father asked Mr. Henley.

"Come over here," Mr. Henley motioned. "Come closer to me. I want to whisper something into your ear."

Father walked over to Mr. Henley, who in a hush-hush voice told him, "Mr. Winkler, what I am going to tell you now is a great secret. I am spending my grandchildren's money."

Every time I reminded Clara of Mr. Henley's boat, she just smiled, and so did I. At the time I am writing these lines, Clara and I have been looking at each other for forty-four years, and we have looked at the sun, the moon and the stars for sixty-two years. We are financially independent. We are happy and healthy. Our children have had a good education. They are all happily married, blessed with their own children, and living in their own homes.

I give credit for all of my accomplishments to my God and to my country. For no other country on the face of this earth crowns hard work, ability and square shooting, with so much abundance, creative of physical comfort.

But what is material success, physical comfort and exterior elegance, without happiness of the heart and the mind and the spiritual peace of the soul? I have found happiness of the heart and the mind in the companionship and the love of the girl I married, and in the pride of accomplishment. I have found spiritual peace of the soul in the process of right thinking, right living and in the memory of my mother, my father and those who so dearly loved me and are now blessed with the peace of eternal rest.

I pray to God that He may grant us the strength to continue wandering, hand in hand, under His sun and the moon and the stars and that He may lengthen our road into that distant rainbow of eternity.

I have nothing but thanks to offer.

If I should ever be born again, I'll gladly go through all of it once more. And if that should ever happen, please God, be sure and let me marry the same girl again.

(1)